The
Sacred Place
of Prayer

Text copyright © Jean Marie Dwyer OP 2013
The author asserts the moral right
to be identified as the author of this work

Published by
The Bible Reading Fellowship
15 The Chambers, Vineyard
Abingdon OX14 3FE
United Kingdom
Tel: +44 (0)1865 319700
Email: enquiries@brf.org.uk
Website: www.brf.org.uk
BRF is a Registered Charity

ISBN 978 0 85746 241 1

First published by Novalis 2011
Publishing Office
10 Lower Spadina Avenue, Suite 400
Toronto, Ontario, Canada
M5V 2Z2
Head Office
4475 Frontenac Street
Montréal, Québec, Canada
H2H 2S2
www.novalis.ca

First UK edition 2013

10 9 8 7 6 5 4 3 2 1 0

Acknowledgments
Unless otherwise stated, scripture quotations are taken from the New Revised Standard
Version of the Bible, Anglicised Edition, copyright © 1989, 1995 by the Division of Christian
Education of the National Council of the Churches of Christ in the United States of America,
and are used by permission. All rights reserved.

The paper used in the production of this publication was supplied by mills that source their
raw materials from sustainably managed forests. Soy-based inks were used in its printing and
the laminate film is biodegradable.

A catalogue record for this book is available from the British Library

Printed in Singapore by Craft Print International Ltd

The Sacred Place of Prayer

The human person created in God's image

Jean Marie Dwyer, OP

Acknowledgments

It is within a community of friendship that we can become most creative and fruitful.

I express my gratitude to my brothers and sisters in the Order who have helped me in this project, and to my monastic community at Queen of Peace, whose encouragement assisted me in giving birth to this work, with particular recognition to Sisters Mary Magdalen, OP, Mary Angela, OP, and Maria Dominica, OP, who have read and reread the chapters. Special gratitude to Sisters Mary Vincent, OP, and Mary Magdalen, OP, members of the Dominican monastery in Farmington Hills, Michigan, for their editing skills, as well as to Father Michael Monshau, OP, who read the manuscript, and Father Thomas McDermott, OP, and Sister Suzanne Noffkke, OP (and Kate, for her prayers), who have encouraged me in this endeavour. I am grateful to my friend Tonia Borkowski, who gave precious feedback from the stance of a Christian layperson, a married woman and mother of five, on the accessibility of the message of this book.

Lastly, I express my profound gratitude to those special sisters and brothers who have accompanied me on this wonderful journey of faith.

Contents

The Mystery of God
and the mystery of
the soul belong together.

Simon Tugwell, OP,
The Beatitudes: Soundings in Christian Traditions

Foreword

Out of the silence of the monastery has come this beautiful book on prayer by Sr Jean Marie, a cloistered Dominican nun. Far from offering a sentimental treatment of the subject or one that is deaf to what our ancestors in the faith have said about prayer, the author has given us an ordered, attractive and personal presentation on the life of prayer that is faithful to life-giving Catholic and Dominican traditions, with taproots deep in scripture and monastic culture.

This is a book for those Christians, whether lay, religious or clergy, who are looking for 'something more' for their spiritual lives, who want occasionally to go beyond prayer of petition—but without leaving it behind. Here is solid food for the soul. We are reminded that we pray not in order to change God's mind or to make God give us something, but to prepare *ourselves* to receive the fullness of divine life found in Jesus Christ. The Holy Spirit, the interior Master of prayer, gradually unites our prayer with the prayer of Christ. As our union with Christ deepens through prayer, the same Spirit assists us in leaving behind our defective ways of thinking and loving so that we may enter more and more into God's thoughts and desires.

Pope Benedict XVI said not long ago that 'believing is beautiful'. *The Sacred Place of Prayer* confirms this truth.

Father Thomas McDermott, OP, author of *Catherine of Siena: Spiritual Development in Her Life and Teaching*

Introduction

I began this book from a desire to share with as many people as possible the great gift of prayer, to show that it is not a complicated set of methods or exercises, but as simple as living life, being ourselves and bringing God into our daily routine. Prayer is a journey, a life-transforming encounter with God. My purpose is to lay the broad contours of a spirituality that empowers us through grace to become 'pray-ers'—to offer a teaching on finding, and entering into, our inner core, where God dwells and we exist in our deepest truth as 'God images'. The focus of my writing is to illustrate the various components we need for life in God, drawing from tradition: scripture, the desert tradition and my own Dominican tradition.

I am a Dominican nun who has lived the monastic tradition for many years. Much of what I write in this book is drawn from years of reflective study, *lectio divina* and my own gradual formation through study and prayerful interaction with the scriptures in community and in solitary prayer. My inspiration for writing is the desire to share with a broader audience the treasures that have nurtured and formed me.

Perhaps what makes my approach to prayer original is my conviction that prayer, even contemplative prayer, is natural to everyone because we are created for God and reflect God. 'There is a mystery at the source of ourselves': in our innermost being we are 'rooted in the mystery of God'.[1] Prayer is a way of life that establishes us in profound communion with God, in whom we are rooted; God, who is the source of our being. Our spiritual journey to holiness is a mystery we enter into; prayer is inseparable from life's journey. Each one of us has our particular timetable of growth in God's plan, yet there are also overarching principles in God's saving action in our lives. It is these principles we seek to share through the witnesses and traditions in this book.

The focus of the book is the human person as the sacred place of prayer. We find this thesis throughout the tradition; I offer only a few of the many sources of this theme. The first three chapters lay philosophical, biblical and theological groundwork for the under-standing of the human person as the sacred place of prayer. Sub-sequent chapters develop this truth more fully. A major premise is that everything flows from our creation in God's image. Each of us is the privileged and sacred place of prayer.

Prayer is meant to shape our whole life, enabling us to become a new creation, to walk with Jesus, to be transformed by conversation with God and to be happy. God's goal for our life is happiness. Our ultimate goal, of course, is to share eternal happiness by entering fully into the life of God—a purpose that is integral to our earthly sojourn. How we live in the world forms us for eternity. Union with God in our daily living produces happiness and security, peace and joy, a joy that is deeper than any sorrow. Jesus promised that we would be filled with a joy that no one can take from us and a peace beyond what the world can understand: 'Peace I leave with you; my peace I give to you. I do not give to you as the world gives' (John 14:27).

The journey, our spiritual adventure, is a healing process that restores and frees our human person in its capacity to be the image of God. Our brokenness and sense of alienation because of sin necessitate our return to the truth of who we are and to the God who dwells within. Learning to be a person of prayer introduces new and wonderful elements into our life: for example, silence and reflection, which in turn can produce an ever-growing sense of awe in being fully alive, fully present not only to God but to ourselves, to creation, to our neighbour and to all the circumstances of life. In a world largely defined by technology and based on philosophies divorced from nature, this is often the last way many experience God.

The first chapter, on Aristotle, sets the tone for the teaching on the human person as the place of prayer. The great philosopher introduces some key principles based on what it means to be human: freedom, natural virtues, true self-love, friendship, with happiness being an essential goal of our humanity. Each subsequent chapter builds on and broadens these basic themes. I have used recurring thoughts and words that are rooted in the scriptures and are classical to the Christian mystical tradition to map out the spiritual journey. Prayer is not just a matter of being spiritual; prayer engages the fullness of our humanity.

We will consider what it means to be a contemplative. The contemplative life does not divorce us from the world or from reality. True contemplative prayer emanating from our innermost centre does not separate us from the real needs of God's people; instead, we become the locus of God's saving action toward the world. This is a truth illustrated in the lives of St Dominic de Guzman and Etty Hillesum, both of whom serve as powerful examples of the effects of prayer in an individual. We will ponder the power of our choices to shape our particular stories. The gift of the God-life and the work of grace are not alien to our human capacity but simply stretch that capacity to its true dimensions.

Throughout the tradition, beginning with the scriptures, love of God and love of neighbour are inseparable. Union with God is impossible without a corresponding oneness with our neighbour (1 John 4:20). Catherine of Siena's teaching explicates this truth in several of the chapters. Perceiving the God image in others, in the weakest of our brothers and sisters, helps us to cherish and love them as other, unselfishly and for themselves.

Much is written today about finding ourselves, knowing ourselves, along with an insatiable desire for love and a place of belonging. The chapters on desert spirituality, illusions and finding our centre give insight into how we find our true self and our place of home and belonging. An inward stillness helps us to seek God in the daily ordinariness of our lives. Setting aside time for prayer is important. Even a momentary pause in a busy day can be an oasis of stillness to re-centre ourselves. Equally important is stilling the unceasing chatter of our thoughts. In a society where noise and distractions are normal fare, such a commitment to silence takes courage. The early monastic tradition clearly understood and taught this truth. No moment, no situation, no pain or misunderstanding can separate us from God's presence, but each one calls us to search more deeply for the face of God.

The last two chapters complete the teaching. First, the chapter on Mary as the place of the new creation brings us into the full revelation of the truth of our existence presented in Genesis. Mary is the sacred space in which the Word of God was conceived. In her openness to God's plan and her response to the Word, we have the model for our discipleship and an illustration for becoming the sacred space for God. The final chapter speaks to us about the source of our prayer, which is the life of God, the life of the Trinity lived in us. We come full circle, beginning with God our Creator and ending with the New Testament revelation of who this God is and how the mystery of God's life is present within us.

The wisdom of the scriptures undergirds the teaching of every chapter. The Genesis text on creation is woven throughout the book. Various spiritual witnesses and traditions show how essential the revealed word of God is for our conversion and transformation. We explore the wisdom of the early desert dwellers. The early monastics were formed by the scriptures and believed in the power of scripture to transform them. They plumbed both the depth of human weakness and our capacity for goodness, love and transformation. Their way of life was essentially following Christ in conformity with the gospel.

The sources of wisdom contained in these pages are diverse, yet the reader will find common threads on the spiritual journey of transformation running through their teachings.

A number of years ago, I decided to learn the Hebrew alphabet. A friend gave me a book with an extremely simple method. The book dedicated about ten pages to one letter, along with one-sentence comments on it. There was no need to memorise, because by the time I had turned the tenth page, I had learned that particular letter. I have used a similar method in writing this book. The one theme of the human person as the place of prayer is visited repeatedly in the various chapters, adding new insights and word descriptions for our understanding as the book progresses. This approach is like looking at a diamond from a variety of enhancing perspectives, allowing the reflected light to bring out the diamond's full beauty.

Prayer is about so many things. It is about God and our relationship with God, but it is also about human relationship, fulfilment and happiness. Learning to pray is about taking time each day to be with God, to be with Jesus, as a friend. Prayer is about opening our hearts to God, being totally truthful before God with all our needs and cares. Prayer is about offering our life to God in praise. It is about speaking to God, but it is even more about creating a still place in our lives and in our hearts where we can hear God speak to us in manifold ways.

The beauty of the world can be a first teacher of prayer. The world is a source of wisdom, since in the beauty and goodness of the world we can find God. If prayer is living life well, in all its truth, then recognising God in creation is the beginning of prayer and an initial step in our relationship with God and with others.

To know God in nature requires stillness, silence and patient waiting. We can capture the face of God in the beauty about us or in the face of another, in a brief moment of insight that fills our hearts with desire for a more prolonged encounter with God. So often, the frantic pace of urban living causes us to miss these quiet, still moments and thus overlook God's presence manifested in our lives. Without silence and reflection we can also fail to grasp the truth that lies at the centre of every human person: that we are a reflection of God's beauty in a unique way, created in the image and likeness of God.

Living a calm, focused life in God's presence does not just affect ourselves: it sends out ripples, shaping the whole universe. Dwelling in God's presence creates harmony and peace in our hearts and in the world. If we were all contemplative, there would be no wars, no strife; rather, the world would be filled with calmness, patience, respect and love. This has been the message of the great Eastern religions for many centuries.

Our world is a broken world because of sin. Because of sin, we lose the sense of God's presence reflected in creation. It is through faith that we come to recognise God in creation. Faith gives us eyes to see with deeper vision, a gift that grows through the ways we exercise it. Faith gives us a wonderful advantage in interpreting both the joys and the sorrows of living. God in Jesus wants us to find and know him, to be taught by the Holy Spirit and to be brought into the infinite love and goodness by which God created us and all things in the beginning.

Contemplative prayer is a gift that God holds out to each one of us. We need only open our heart to receive the fullness of the divine mystery of love.

Perhaps, as you read these pages, you will discover that prayer is so much more than you thought. My hope is that this discovery may continue, deepen and be the beginning and end of all you do in life. Take time for wonder and awe at small things, at existence, at life, at the love we can share with one another. It opens the door to God.

Part 1

Creation: the beginning

Life's journey of prayer

Begun long ago, traversing many paths
How often have I stood at crossroads?
How often felt the movement of the Spirit
deep within—calling?
Why this persistent voice
ruffling my inner complacency?
Life's journey, light and darkness,
the movement of the heart
leading to the deepest centre
of home, of belonging.
Every whisper a new dying
and paradoxically new life.
Leaving behind something that seemed
so essential to being, yet not so.
Desert wandering, an emptiness
yet joyous openness of space—
where empty expanse offers clarity of sight.
The desert of our spiritual journey
in the beginning a pathless landscape
that calls for measureless trust and hope.
Where is home and belonging?
There is light—One who speaks.
And I will follow—
I will walk through each open door
of the inner chamber of my heart.
God is there and I—in all my truth.

1
In the beginning: Aristotle

We get [virtues] by first exercising them... For the things we have to learn before we can do them we learn by doing them.[2]

'In the beginning... God created...' (Genesis 1:1). This is the beginning of every story, the answer to all the questions and the beginning of all beginnings. It is also the beginning and development of this book on prayer. Where is the place of prayer? The true place of prayer is not just about space or posture. I believe that the true place of prayer is the human person, created in God's image. Prayer is about a relationship with God and, in God, with each of our sisters and brothers and all God's creation. Prayer is a fire of love that transforms us, a love that leads us into God and then proceeds outward in love to others.

The human person turned toward the divine

The Greek philosopher Aristotle (384–322BC) came to the conclusion that there was a spark of the divine in the deepest centre of each man and woman. His wisdom touches some vital truths about human beings that God's revelation illuminates more completely. Aristotle's thoughts on the universe and the human person—who and what we are, the life of virtue, happiness and freedom—ground us firmly in understanding the human person as the sacred place of prayer.

Our purpose for this chapter is a modest one. It does not offer an exhaustive exposition of Aristotle's philosophy or the effect that philosophies have on our thinking and action, though philosophy does direct our individual lives and gives form to the culture in which we live. Aristotle's writing has had immeasurable influence on human thought and civilisation. But we must be satisfied with using only a few of his key insights from the *Nicomachean Ethics* for our study. (References in the text are drawn from the *Ethics*.)

Aristotle questions the meaning of life. He reflects upon the gifts inherent in our nature. His questions are the ones that dwell in the heart of every human being: questions about life, happiness, good and evil, suffering, ultimate meaning and destiny. To reflect on such questions—indeed, reflection itself—lies at the heart of our humanness. Aristotle's definitions of virtue and contemplation and some of his other intuitions do not reach the fullness of Christian revelation, but they are a dim foreshadowing of this fullness, even while his theories are deficient and limited.

Every human being is limited, as is every age and system of thought. The greatest of us is limited. Our limitedness brings home to us that we are created to be interdependent. We are social beings in need of one another. Aristotle understood this truth. He teaches that we are not meant to live in isolation but in a society where ideally we seek the common good of all. This is an essential part of what human happiness is all about, as is our individuality. That the human person is unique, an individual, separate from every other human person, conveys that there also exists within each of us a gift of solitude.

Aristotle taught that the human person is relational. Friendship is necessary for human happiness. Friendship is characterised by loving rather than being loved and by desiring ultimate goodness and happiness for the friend (*Ethics*, Book VIII.8, p. 205). In the *Ethics* he lists several types of friendship, such as sharing a common project with another, or having common interests, but he considers the highest experience of friendship to be between two people who love each other for one another's good. A friendship built on virtue is an enduring and equal bond between two people (Book VIII.13, p. 217).

Aristotle addresses an interesting point when he writes that real friendship is based upon self-love (Book IX.4, pp. 227–230). Self-love is not the same as an introspective, selfish love, but is a healthy understanding of the uniqueness of our person, our value and our dignity. Selfishness produces isolation, while self-love creates relationship. If we cannot love ourselves, then our love and respect for others will be hindered. Only a good person is able to find and cultivate the good in another; only the virtuous person is able to possess truth and virtue and perceive and sustain the truth and virtue in another (Book IX.4, pp. 227ff).

Aristotle's conclusions have touched on several important elements needed for prayer: relationship and solitude rather than isolation, mature self-love, and love for the other blossoming into friendship. The capacity to love is essential for prayer.

Nature: the gift of being

Aristotle wrote on the meaning and purpose of the universe and all its various inhabitants. His philosophy begins with reality: real things such as trees and water, you and me, politics, and the environment in which we live. His primary textbook was life itself: the workings of the human mind, creation, and the interaction of human beings with one another. He came to profound insights about human life and happiness.

His *Ethics* is built on a philosophy of nature, that things are what they are, possessing certain innate characteristics. Dogs, cats, plants, stones and human beings each possess characteristics that are essential to their particular nature. These characteristics are not acquired by experience but arise from the basic structure of what makes a plant a plant, a cat a cat, and a human person a human person. Human beings possess certain inherent traits; it is also true to say that our experiences shape the unique person we are, the well-known combination of nature and nurture.

Aristotle's concept of the 'good life' is based on what it means to be human. Human beings share a common destiny and purpose: happiness. The good life is the life in which every person has a right by nature to certain goods: food, clothing, shelter and enough material possessions to live with dignity, along with the freedom to be reflective, acquire knowledge, make choices, be respected and esteemed, and love and enjoy friendship. Every human person, in the gift of his or her existence, is meant to be happy, free and uniquely esteemed and respected. A Greek pagan philosopher came to these conclusions, using the wonderful gifts of nature with which he was endowed. Christianity affirms these basic truths of what it means to be human and goes much further, revealing to us the height and breadth and depth of human happiness as God's gift of abundant life.

The life of virtue

One of the stepping stones for our study is Aristotle's teaching on virtue. The Greek word he uses for 'virtue' means 'excellence' (*Ethics*, Translator's Preface, p. xxvi). He defines moral virtue as an excellence of character (Book II.6, p. 36). Living a virtuous life consists in forming good habits by making practical choices. Human excellence lies in choosing the good (Book II.6, pp. 39ff). How do we know what is good according to this great philosopher? He would answer that the good lies in the nature of the thing: if this nature is not thwarted, there is a dynamism within that moves it toward perfection. The fulfilment of the purpose for which a thing exists is its good and its truth.

Aristotle teaches that virtue lies in the middle way between extremes: a right judgment in seeking the good, in the correct measure with the right priorities (Book II.6, p. 38). Thomas Aquinas calls this 'prudence'. Moral virtue is about the ability to make right choices. Our choices are embedded in particular situations and set against a broader background, which Aristotle would call the ultimate goal of human activity. Moral activity forms our judgments and our understanding of the good. There are both subjective and objective elements in the formation of human judgment.

We learn virtue by choosing what is good and rejecting what is bad. An example is how we choose to spend our time, or whose company we keep. What our choices are directed toward forms the kind of person we are. Reflective choices are essential to moral activity. A virtuous person is one whose morally good choices have become ingrained, like the air we breathe; consequently, virtue becomes easy. Right choices in life create habits that turn us more easily to what is good and true. The stronger the habits we develop, the greater the ease with which we act.

Freedom to choose the good defines human existence and belongs to us as a fundamental component of who we are. It is not the freedom that is so often spoken about in our modern Western society—a freedom to be without limits. This view of freedom is connected to the 'right' of the individual to do whatever she or he wants, almost irrespective of whether these actions hurt or help others. Freedom defined in this way creates isolation and is far removed from the social nature that Aristotle thought gave definition to human existence. When we look at the story of Adam and Eve in the book of Genesis, it is clear that human beings are created social and that isolation is a fruit of sin and separation from God.

Formed by desire

We are formed by the desires that move us toward the choices we make. Aristotle distinguishes between real human needs and those things we want. The former are the goods inherently and absolutely necessary for human fulfilment; the latter are what we could call our wish list, those things that can make life better. We can want so many things. It is certainly a good to live above mere subsistence. Our society is in a sad state because a few possess wealth far exceeding their needs, and thus a majority must exist without even what is necessary for happiness and human flourishing.

Possessing everything we want is not always what gives us happiness; having more, having in excess, often prevents us from enjoying or appreciating true happiness and can even prevent a growth in freedom. If one person amasses wealth and possessions to the detriment of his neighbour, he is not seeking the common good. Our consumer society certainly testifies to this truth. In a world where the dignity of each person is not respected, where the goods of the earth are not shared, we have injustice, poverty and oppression—the exact opposite of what Aristotle considered moral excellence to be. Inordinate wants stifle our freedom.

How does Aristotle perceive truth? He presents a very practical understanding in the *Nicomachean Ethics*, which will serve us well as we consider prayer. Truth is, for Aristotle, the integrity of the person in the face of life's situations. A person of integrity is 'truthful both in life and in word' (Book IV.7, p. 101). Aristotle's definition of truth is close to that of the Old Testament, where truthfulness has to do with honesty, justice and right relations with our neighbour, which reflect God's loving kindness to us. Truth is not an abstract proposition held only in the mind; rather, truth is about good living where there is accord between what one speaks and how one lives. Some of the wisdom teaching that follows will elaborate on this meaning of truth.

Living the good life

Human beings are reflective by nature. We need to reflect in order to live life well. Aristotle equated being fully reflective with contemplation. To live our lives without thought of what we are doing, or where we are going, or what is essential, is not to realise our full potentiality.

Aristotle believed that there should be a plan to our life, that there are goals toward which human beings move and there are means to help us attain these goals.[3] We need to step back periodically to ponder where our life is leading, what we are really seeking and whether we are going in the right direction. Silence and space to reflect are important and necessary for our human maturation and for growth in our love for God and for one another. According to Aristotle, peace and stability in the face of the misfortunes of life are the fruits of a life of moral excellence (Book X.6, pp. 261–263).

On contemplation

Finally, let us briefly explore Aristotle's thought on the human person as contemplative. He taught that the use of reason and the pursuit of wisdom reached their climax in contemplation, which he saw as the fullest realisation of human potentiality and the final purpose of human action (Book X.7 and 8, pp. 288–295). Here Aristotle is talking about a natural contemplation that resides in our human powers to reason. His philosophy did not reach the understanding of the human person as created by God, sustained and perfected by the gift of grace. Aristotle held out little hope for those who were defective either in upbringing or in their mental capacity. Yet through God's revelation, we know that every person is an image of God, precious, touched by God's love and destined for glory. God has gifted us with a natural capacity for vision, for perceiving the beauty, goodness and truth of reality. This is a gift given not to a few elite, but to everyone. This vision is a participation in the divine. In the contemplative life, we taste the beginning of eternity.

Aristotle thought of contemplation as something that people attained by training and discipline, but also as a gift of the gods. Contemplation enables the human person to participate in the one activity that can be attributed to the gods themselves. We have within us something divine that fulfils our human capacity while, at the same time, going beyond it. According to Aristotle, in our ability to reflect and understand the truth of reality, the human person most nearly approaches divine blessedness. For him, the power to reason and to be reasonable is a divine principle in human nature, and so a life lived in accordance with reason would also be divine.[4]

Conclusion

Aristotle's philosophy in itself is a testimony to our ability to reflect and be contemplative. He built his thought on the Greek thinkers who went before him. He believed that everything exists for a purpose. Our purposefulness is found within the dynamism of our existence, in what he considered a natural impulse toward perfection.

Although Aristotle never reached the truth of a personal God who created us, his lofty human reflection reaches completion in the revealed truth of the scriptures. Our natural gift of being reflective and contemplative, as Aristotle understood it, becomes a building block for understanding our absolute dignity as persons created in God's image and likeness.

Aristotle's understanding of virtue as the way to happiness is one of the lasting truths imparted to future ages. His philosophy is profound, even astounding, though incomplete. God's revelation of creation in the light of its relation to the Creator was needed for the fullness of truth that this great philosopher sought. In his philosophy, Aristotle intuited those fundamental human gifts that, scripture reveals, are received from God at our creation.

The beginning of wisdom is the understanding that everything has its own dimensions, its own truth. Aristotle built his philosophy on such principles. To live virtuously, to be free, truly free to choose goodness, is to break our hearts wide open to the gift of love, to the gift of being in God and toward the other, and to allow ourselves to become the place of prayer.

Reflections

On being reflective

Inward attentiveness to reality allows us to have a broader perspective and a deeper understanding of the events of life, our desires and the direction in which we are moving. Make time for periods of silence to reflect on the beauty of creation, on your life, on the past, on the present reality and on future hopes in the light of God's plan for you.

What things would you like to change in your life? What events, circumstances and people are having the greatest influence on your life? Is their influence good or bad? What steps do you think you need to take to direct your future in the way most conducive to a life of virtue and Godliness? Make a list of specific and concrete suggestions.

2

Prayer and the wisdom of salvation in scripture

The essential source of my identity is God. There is really only one source of life in us, and that is fully human only in being also divine.[5]

God's Word is an overarching theme of this book. God's Word refers to the second person of the Trinity, to the revelation of the scriptures, and to the ultimate revelation of God in Jesus, who entered into our humanity. The Word of God is an encounter with God, the ultimate source of our salvation.

The Bible teaches us that listening to God and following in his way is the path to wisdom and leads to happiness. The path to life and happiness is mapped out by God and consists in learning to be God-like. We find true freedom in living a life modelled on God's attributes: goodness, oneness, simplicity and love.

The Wisdom literature of the Old Testament tells us that everything begins with 'fear of the Lord'. This is not a subservient fear of punishment but reverential fear, the recognition of our fundamental dependency on God for our very existence. The revelation of God's nature reveals to us our nature; it unveils for us the meaning of the human person. In knowing God, we come to know ourselves. Human beings come forth from God's goodness.

God's wisdom in the Old Testament uses the medium of human words and stories. God reveals himself in human words that make known to us how we are to be God-like. In this revelation, God, through the voice of the human author, describes the otherness of his being in anthropomorphic terms so that we may apply these images to ourselves and be divinised. God walks with Adam and Eve, and we are to walk with God. God is just and righteous, a God of forgiveness who sees his people's sins and forgives them. Likewise, we are called to mirror God's righteousness and forgiveness to others. God signs a contract of faithfulness with us, that we may reciprocate in a covenantal bond with God.

The Old Testament is filled with stories about people just like us, saints and sinners, who have been called by God to freedom and holiness. God created us to participate in the divine life for all eternity: our completion as human beings can be attained only in faithfulness to our created essence, as made in the image and likeness of God. There is within each of us a movement toward eternity and God, who is our beginning and our end. God created us with the capacity for freedom, which we can use to respond to God's wisdom or turn away and follow our own paths. God's gift of freedom makes us capable of choosing good or evil. The stories in the Old Testament are about both choices: 'I have set before you life and death, blessings and curses. Choose life so that you and your descendants may live, loving the Lord your God, obeying him, and holding fast to him; for that means life to you and length of days' (Deuteronomy 30:19–20).

God reveals himself and his plan in the stories and actions of key men and women of the Old Testament. Think of Adam and Eve, Noah, Abraham and Sarah, Moses and the prophets. The ways their lives are laid out teach us and future generations about the goodness and sinfulness of those whom God calls to follow him. In the actions of Israel as a people, we can learn similar wisdom. In the story of Israel we have the paradigm for God's sanctifying journey with each of us. It is a story of healing and unconditional love in the face of betrayal, weakness and sin. We see in this history the way God guides his people on a journey.

The journey is both spatial, a journey to a place, and a movement of the heart: inward toward spiritual transformation and outward toward communion.

The first creation: divine likeness

Genesis contains two different but theologically complementary stories of the creation of human beings. God created all things by his Word and breathed into them the life of his Spirit. God began creation with nothing but his own being. In some mysterious way, everything that was made came forth from God and reflected his essence. Creation is not God, but reflects God. Human beings reflect God in a unique manner. God breathed into human beings a special likeness to the divine essence, imparting to us a share in the trinitarian love and knowledge. We are created in the image of God. Prayer flows from our relationship to God, who is the ground of our existence.

The two creation stories in Genesis teach what is essential to being human. Our rationality as thinking, reflective creatures sets us apart as sharing in the reflective wisdom and knowledge of God. The rationality of human beings is also the source of our stewardship over the rest of God's creation, a stewardship meant to be an image of God's benign and loving presence to all creation. The second account of creation in chapter 2 of Genesis makes it clear that human beings are created relational. It is part of our very existence to be turned toward the other, God and our neighbour. The Lord God had created the man and put him in the garden. 'Then the Lord God said, "It is not good that the man should be alone; I will make him a helper as his partner"' (Genesis 2:18).

The story of sin

From the story of humankind's subsequent fall, we learn about sin, brokenness, duplicity and hiding ourselves from God, realities we encounter in ourselves and in our dealings with others: 'God called to the man, and said to him, "Where are you?" He said, "I heard the sound of you in the garden, and I was afraid, because I was naked; and I hid myself." He said, "Who told you that you were naked?"' (Genesis 3:9–11).

In the temptation story (3:1–7), God's gift of divine likeness and sharing in divine knowledge is subtly manipulated: 'Your eyes will be opened, and you will be like God' (v. 5). In submitting, their eyes were opened and they saw themselves in their nakedness and vulnerability. Fear entered into their hearts—a fear generated by a sense of alienation from God—so they hid themselves. The modern frantic search for identity speaks eloquently about how well we continue to hide. God formed and knows our innermost being; nothing can be hidden from his knowledge (Psalm 139:7–16). Human beings created as essentially relational now find themselves isolated because of sin. As human history progresses, loneliness haunts the human spirit.

Adam and Eve sought a knowledge of themselves that was outside God's will for them. The tempter holds out a gift of being 'like God' that is other than the perfect gift of likeness that was already given in our creation. The temptation is subtle because it is close to the truth: 'God knows that when you eat of [the fruit] your eyes will be opened, and you will be like God, knowing good and evil' (3:5).

The knowledge that they received was the negative truth of their separateness from God, from the truth of who they were as participators in the divine life. Sin revealed the truth of existence outside God. So began our history of estrangement from God, from our true selves as God-bearers and from our neighbour.

Knowledge, understanding and love are linked throughout the scriptures. God wants us to know him so that we may love him. We need to allow God's knowledge of us to enlighten our self-knowledge in order to arrive at the truth of who we are.

God's intervention and saving action

The language of the flood story (Genesis 6—9) echoes that of the first creation and points to God's will to save us from our sins. It is another creation story and emblematic of God's continued faithfulness. It is also a symbolic representation of God's new creation in Christ, where sin and evil are definitively destroyed. The story of the flood is the story of God's intervention and will to save. In rechoosing the various creatures, male and female, to repopulate the earth, God again utters the original mandate to human beings: 'Be fruitful and multiply, and fill the earth' (9:1).

God's choice of Abraham and Abraham's journey to the promised land form the model of our journey into spiritual transformation: 'Go from your country and your kindred and your father's house to the land that I will show you' (Genesis 12:1). It is about the journey inward and then outward toward the Other/other; a movement from the land of unlikeness to likeness. Transformation usually entails a movement away from the known and the comfortable into that which we are to become: a new creation in Christ.

In Christ, God's perfect image

The New Testament authors build on this initial revelation of the Old Testament: that we are made in God's image as relational beings, but because of sin we are weak and in need of God's healing grace.

In the beginning God created all things in his Word and breathed life into creation through his Spirit—in Hebrew, *ruah*, 'God's breath'. The prologue of John's Gospel echoes the creation story, emphasising that all things were created in God's Word, and then identifying Jesus as that Word. Our definitive re-creation is effected in God's sending the Son, his Word spoken now in such a way that God became one of us. Jesus teaches us that God who is One is also relational, a triune reciprocal relation of eternal love. Thus we are brought into a deeper understanding of our created communion with one another as an image of God's triune essence.

In many places in the New Testament teaching, we are confronted with our need for healing and redemption. Healing comes with our entering into an imitation of Jesus and opening our hearts to the purifying illumination of the Holy Spirit, who is the Spirit of Jesus (Ephesians 4:4–16). There are many wonderful ways to follow these themes through the scriptures and to see how the New Testament teaching continues and fulfils the theology of the Old Testament.

The overwhelming message of both the Old and New Testaments is that God's call and abundant self-giving love necessitate a response of self-giving surrender and love on our part.

God's word: in the believing community

God continues to speak to us through the scriptures. For Christians, the Old and New Testaments stand as the totality of God's revelation to his people. The word of God continues to be alive and active, transforming the mind and the heart. The liturgy of the church, in a unique way, is the place of the verbal communication of God's word. As we listen with faith and receptivity, God in Christ and through the power of the Holy Spirit transforms the believer and the believing community. We meet Christ in this exceptional way in the daily eucharistic celebration and in praying the Liturgy of the Hours; both are the action of Christ and the action of the praying church.

Today: the day of salvation

The scriptures introduce the immediacy of the transforming power of listening and responding to the word of God proclaimed in the gathering of the people through the concept of 'today'. Today is the day of the Lord. For Israel, rereading their history in the midst of the assembly is not something that happened in the past but is present now (see Nehemiah 8:1–6). It is new today, a new word, and a new experience for this assembly. The word's power to transform is now. God's grace comes to us in the present moment. Today, this moment, is the defining timeframe of our existence. Today is the moment to open our hearts: 'O that today you would listen to his voice! Do not harden your hearts' (Psalm 95:7–8).

In Deuteronomy 26:16–19, the word 'today' is like a mantra that Moses calls out to the people over and over again. *Today* God calls you to obey the command; *today* God has entered into an agreement with you; *today* God has made you to be a people holy to the Lord.

We catch this same sense of vibrancy and the immediacy of faith in the gathering of the early church; for example, in the proclamation of the good news, the apostles were so filled with the joy of the Holy Spirit that they were thought to be drunk (Acts 2:13). The timelessness of the events of salvation, re-enacted in the liturgy, have for us the same immediacy that the word had for Israel and the early church. Think of the Christmas carol 'O come, all ye faithful', in which we sing (only on Christmas Day itself), 'Yea, Lord, we greet thee, born this happy morning.'

The church, in its liturgical celebration with the public reading of the scriptures and in its sacramental life, continues to call us to a vibrant response to God's word. The eucharistic celebration and the reading of God's word should not leave us unaffected; each encounter can bring us more fully into an experience of transformation, truly making us alive to God's call.

In the liturgical cycle of seasons and ordinary time, the celebration of the word opens for our understanding the history of Israel as the story of our salvation. Through participation in the liturgy, we respond to God's saving work. This truth is highlighted during the seasons of Advent and Lent, culminating in the feast of feasts, Easter, when the scriptures impart the plan of God in its wisdom. We are called to share in this wisdom by our response of faith and joyful surrender.

Living prayer

Both our union with God and our ongoing response to the divine initiative are the basis for prayer. In order to pray well, we need to enter progressively more profoundly into the mystery of God. Our union with God is not isolated to certain times of the day, but encompasses the transformation of our whole being by grace. What we do, the choices we make, flows from that radical transformation.

Above all, scripture teaches us that prayer is about our union with God, in Jesus and through the Holy Spirit. Prayer encompasses all we are, which perfects in us the divine likeness so that indeed we shall be like God.

It is Jesus who is the perfect likeness of God; we are being transformed into Jesus for God's glory. Thus, scripture links the wisdom of God's way of salvation and the transforming power of prayer as the moment of encounter with God that goes beyond that moment to bring every moment of our living into God's presence.

Reflections

Living with silence and a focus on God

Take some time each day to be free of media noise: TV, iPods, internet, and so on. Try to capture what it means to be silent. Take a silent walk or sit in silence. Perhaps the biggest challenge is to be comfortable being silent with someone else or with a group. Throughout the day, recall a word or phrase from scripture or some other spiritual source to refocus yourself in God.

3

St Catherine of Siena: iconographer of prayer

You, eternal Trinity, are the craftsman; and I your handiwork have come to know that you are in love with the beauty of what you have made… You have made of me a new creation in the blood of your Son. [6]

St Catherine was born in Siena, Italy, on 25 March 1347. She was the 24th of 25 children. Her family lived near the Dominican Church of San Domenico, a centre of Dominican preaching and teaching. She entered the Mantellate, a group for women affiliated with the Order of St Dominic who lived at home and ministered to the poor and the sick. Catherine lived in very turbulent times for the church; she sought to bring the Pope back to Rome, and succeeded for a short time. She died on 29 April 1380, at Rome. In 1970, Paul VI declared Catherine of Siena and Teresa of Avila the first women Doctors of the Church.

Catherine of Siena's doctrine flows from her mystical experience of God. She is an iconographer of the spiritual life who creates beautiful and insightful images. Although her mystical images are particular, the truths they express are universal. In the writings of the saints there is always a broad, general prototype that God uses for everyone, and a unique pattern manifested in the life of this particular mystic. Because Catherine has been declared a Doctor of the Church, we know that her teachings offer something for everyone.

God frequently reveals himself to us through prayer images. The saints testify to this truth. St Catherine's mysticism is built upon prayer images: God as a mirror, Jesus as the bridge, the steps of contemplation, the sea, fire and many others. Prayer images are like parables; they contain many layers of meaning that unfold as we reflect on their content in prayer. That is why images are so appropriate for understanding our contemplative experiences of God. God helps the individual to recognise his will through these imaginative visitations. God, who is beyond our senses, manifests himself through the symbolism of prayer images.

Catherine was a woman of wisdom. She is a practical guide in understanding prayer as rooted in our human reality. Scripture tells us that eternal life is to 'know... God, and Jesus Christ whom [he has] sent' (John 17:3). This is why Catherine can speak of such an intimate possession of God even in this life. Her faith is reflected in her mystical experiences, her words and her actions. Integrity of word, life and action speak of a harmony within the person. Where this harmony is found there is holiness and a re-creation, a 'restored' humanity.

The human person as the image of God

Catherine's teaching on the human person is positive: our goodness and beauty come from our creation in God's image and likeness. In her prayer, Catherine asks why God created us. What moved him to enlighten us in his truth? She writes, 'You [God], yourself, the very fire of love, *you yourself are the reason* (*The Dialogue*, p. 273, author's emphasis). She writes that 'love is the stuff' we are made of because God created us through love (*The Dialogue*, pp. 104, 49). What a wonderful understanding of our humanity!

I am who I am

The spiritual journey begins for Catherine with an understanding of the gift of her existence. It is important to grasp this truth at the beginning of the spiritual journey, because it is also the truth of the end of the journey: participation in the triune life of God. 'Do you know, daughter, who you are and who I am? If you know these two things, you will be blessed. You are she who is not; whereas I am he who is.'[7]

This initial revelation produces in Catherine a profound understanding of who she is and who God is: creature to Creator. The recognition of our creatureliness is the ground for humility and receptive openness to our continued giftedness from God. The spiritual journey to which Catherine leads us is first an inward one, in order to understand what it means to be created in the image of God. Our consummate truth as human persons is that we are, in our very creation, God-like.

God is the root of our essence. Our existence complements the divine existence, as a mirror reflecting in some small portion God's essence. In the light of God's *allness*, God's revelation to Catherine that 'you are she who is not' is not negative but a sign of the overwhelming love and goodness of God, who has created us as a reflection of the divine goodness. We can rejoice in the gift of our existence and every gift of grace bestowed upon us because God is our life (*The Dialogue*, p. 144).

Knowing ourselves in God

In the gentle mirror of God she sees her own dignity: that through no merit of hers, but by his creation, she is the image of God. And in the mirror of God's goodness she sees as well her own unworthiness, the work of her own sin. (The Dialogue, p. 48)

Catherine's description of God as the gentle mirror is a significant image. God is the gentle mirror in which we see ourselves reflected through the prism of God's mercy and compassion. We see and know ourselves through the icon of God's merciful love. This image says so much about our journey to God and God's steadfast love and patient mercy.

As we come to know God, we also learn to know ourselves in truth. It is a double-faceted truth: the truth that we reflect God's being in a profound, yet mysterious way, and the truth of our sin and unworthiness. Our reflected image in God's mirror is always positive and healing, whether we see his grace at work in us or our own sinfulness. Knowing ourselves in God helps us to understand our real dignity.

Paul teaches that we console others with the same consolation with which God consoled us (2 Corinthians 1:4). Therefore our human need and fragility become the gracious encounter with the other where God's love and compassion are mirrored in our loving-kindness, mercy and forgiveness. Perceiving ourselves in the mirror of God's mercy, we become a mirror of God's mercy and love to others. Many of the pervading cultural biases of our time have lost sight of the basic goodness of the human person. Catherine's perception of God as a mirror in which we look for our true face is a wonderful insight for our identity-seeking culture.

A true knowledge of ourselves can only be attained in a reciprocal knowledge of God's love for us and his goodness to us as Creator and lover, desiring to draw us back to ourselves. For Catherine, the spiritual journey is a return to the inward truth of our real dignity as human beings: the journey out of our sinfulness to that primal state of emptiness where it is God who re-creates and fills us with all that we are. The knowledge of God and the knowledge of self season one another.

Desire

Catherine gave a central place to desire in her teaching on the spiritual life: 'I repay every labour and fulfil holy desires whenever I find people knocking in truth and with light at the door of my mercy, so that they may not stray or falter in their hope in my providence' (*The Dialogue*, p. 100).

Our desires for God, for goodness, for prayer, and our yearning to become whole and free, are signs of the work of the Holy Spirit within. These desires of our heart and the movement of the Holy Spirit within are always more layered than we can understand. Discernment, then, is a movement toward understanding the meaning of God's call at this moment, along with a commitment of trust, allowing the Holy Spirit to take us beyond the moment into God's vision for us. The metaphors of thirst and desire are often synonymous in our spiritual journey. The content of our thirst/desire is an inner word, a clue to God's grace at work in us. Because we are made in God's image, the core of our being, which is united to the Holy Spirit, seeks to enter into God's gift of transformation. Sin and the ways in which life has wounded us do not define who we are unless we choose to reject God irrevocably. We need only listen to God who dwells within us and let go to be healed and transformed.

God reveals to Catherine that, in creating us in his image, God gave us the gift of memory to hold fast the remembrance of his gifts. Memory enables us to hold in our mind's eye our moments of light during times of darkness; during times of light, we remember the grace of God's strength sustaining us in our times of darkness. Life, for all of us, is a journey through light and darkness. God is present to us both in times of joy, when God is palpably near, and in times of sorrow, darkness, suffering, pain and loss, when God seems absent. The alternating patterns of light and darkness in our life can bring us to a confident trust that God is never absent, but is near whatever the circumstances of our life, through his love and sustaining power.

Re-creation in Christ and through the Holy Spirit

We lost grace through Adam's sin and were restored by the coming of Jesus into our world. God restored the divine image in human beings by becoming human, one like us in everything but sin (*The Dialogue*, pp. 46–47). We are a new creation in the blood of Jesus and re-established in grace. God's loving mercy accompanies us when we are weak and fragile.

Catherine uses the image of the bridge to explain the incarnation—the linking of heaven and earth through Jesus' taking on our humanity. She writes, 'Though the living bridge [Jesus] has been taken from your sight, there remains the bridgeway of his teaching, which is held together by my power and my Son's wisdom and the mercy of the Holy Spirit. *My power gives the virtue of courage to those who follow his way*' (*The Dialogue*, p. 70, author's emphasis).

The Holy Spirit is the love of God dwelling within us, a love that strengthens us to manifest God's work and truth. 'True love casts out all fear' (*The Dialogue*, p. 119). Fearlessness to live in the truth is a sign of perfect love abiding in our hearts. Such fearlessness was the experience of the disciples after Pentecost.

Christ opened the way for us to enter into the cycle of the trinitarian life. Again we have access to God's original plan of love for creation. In Jesus and through the sanctifying love of the Holy Spirit, we return to the Father. This is our spiritual journey. Catherine teaches us that it is an inward journey to our innermost part and then an outward journey to include our neighbour.

Conclusion

God invites us to enter into the heart of the divine, to live within the mystery of God and to experience the power of God's healing and redeeming work. It is in God that 'we live and move and have our being' (Acts 17:28). Jesus, who is God, took on the simple daily routines of our life and connected them to the dizzying height that Catherine describes.

Jesus came among us precisely to take upon himself human love and human compassion, human weakness, the effects of sin and death itself. This is indeed love! The way we return to God is by passing through the everyday events of life, our weakness, our woundedness and our sin, in such a way that all becomes grace. It is a gradual, day-by-day process.

Life is the arena where we learn to be Jesus, where we learn to love; in loving and serving our neighbour, we really understand what it means to be divine.

God asks us to step out beyond ourselves and be clothed anew in his vision for our life. God is always the God of surprises. He gifts us with many wonderful moments of knowledge and love, then asks us to translate them into living the very ordinary circumstances of our life where we can share his giftedness with others.

What are we passionate about? It is our passions that drive us to action. Being passionate is a gift. It helps us to run the course with intensity and openness. In connection with holiness and godliness, being passionate is a gift of vital importance. As Catherine affirms, it puts a fire into our heart that moves us to reach out to the fullness of grace—not tomorrow, but now, in the eternal now of the present moment.

Reflections

Prayer images and sacred images

In the silence of prayer, picture a symbol of your prayer or spiritual need, a word picture: for example, resting in God, forgiveness, or an image from nature—a tree, mountains, the sea. It is important to use our imagination in prayer—to picture our journey with the Lord in symbols.

Here is a prayer image of repentance I have used: 'I saw myself standing before God as a little child, dirty and bedraggled, offering a humble daisy, a small offering for all the day's failings.'

Rest in the image without words. Trust yourself to the infinite love of God that surrounds you in the silence.

Part 2
Becoming the place of prayer

Lump of clay on potter's wheel
unshaped and formless,
filled with the density of its own clayness.
In the hands of the Master Potter
shaped and hollowed,
reforming its clayness to glory.
Nothing is lost, only new dimensions given it.
Its clayness realised in full potential
as a vessel shaped for glory.
A hollowed vessel of Mercy,
itself an empty space
which is a true dimension
of its being, as created.
Fragile clay imparted
Potter's dream and shape.
A vessel hallowed and shaped,
an empty/fullness of giftedness
for oneself and for others.
Once lump of clay dense
and strong in its own density.
Now fragile vessel of clay
shaped to beauty,
its own and the gift of another.

4

Desert spirituality: becoming a Godly space

Through prayer, therefore, it is brought about that a heart is turned toward him who is always ready to give, provided we are ready to accept whatever he may give.[8]

In the early fourth and fifth centuries, at a time when there was no longer widespread persecution and the church had grown complacent, men and women ascetics fled into the deserts of Egypt, Syria, Palestine and Arabia. The great centre of this early monastic movement was the desert of Egypt. These men and women withdrew from mainstream society and culture as a way of following Jesus and living the gospel. They undertook a radical commitment of discipleship, entering into a process of healing and restoration. They lived as hermits in caves and in huts and finally in formal communities of monks founded by Pachomius. The desert was peppered with their huts.

As the desert became more populated, these ascetics moved deeper into the wilderness seeking solitude. By our standards they were a rough group and led a life of great asceticism. Yet they did not define themselves by asceticism but by living a life of charity. They were seeking God, and the way to God is through love. 'The gentle charity of the desert was the pivot of all their work and the test of their way of life.'[9] Both men (Abbas) and women (Ammas) entered the desert, but the men far outnumbered the women—

although the asceticism of the Ammas was as great as that of the monks.

Journey, movement and place are special themes that we want these early followers of Jesus, and masters of prayer, to teach us. Their journey is common to all who seek God in the grace of Jesus. For these men and women, the desert was the place to search for and realise communion with God. We find our own deserts in the circumstances of our life. Their wisdom helps us to understand some of the common elements in God's call. The way to holiness is personal to each one of us. Yet there is a commonality in the need for a commitment to follow God's call, and in the necessity of purification to prepare us for grace and conversion, leading to transformation.

These ancient desert dwellers understood the wilderness as a place for refocusing, for getting things into perspective, for removing obstacles to living in God. They sought the desert as a place of silence and emptiness, free from all that obscures the essentials of the God journey. The wisdom they learned in the desert can teach us the indispensable contours of prayer and relationship with God. The texts frequently reiterate what were seen as the virtues of the desert: 'humility, discretion, realism, the "single eye" of a life directed toward God'.[10]

When we speak about the movement into the desert, we are referring to a dual movement. The barren terrain is a space conducive to the radical undertaking of conversion. It was also the place of encounter with the desert of the human heart in its sinful and wounded condition. Our hearts are the place where God abides, often initially hidden from us under many layers of experiences that have coloured our sense of self and of God.[11] 'This confluence of topology and spiritual longing recurs throughout the literature of early Christian monasticism... the desert is identified as the place of the heart.'[12]

Paradise regained

The encounter with God's word in the sacred scripture formed the Desert Fathers and Mothers. In fact, their life in the desert was seen as a continuation of God's saving history. They pondered the creation story of Genesis and understood that God created the human person in the image and likeness of God. Scripture tells us that God saw his creation as good. Thus, human beings and all creation are fundamentally good. The great asceticism of the desert was never a denial of the basic goodness of the human person, but rather a response to the hold that sin and weakness have on the human heart without grace.

A recurring theme in the literature about the desert dwellers is the recovery of paradise and that first innocence possessed by Adam and Eve.[13] To regain paradise meant to enter into a process of healing. The monks were convinced that the asceticism of the journey would make them free and restore the inner peace and tranquillity possessed by Adam and Eve, along with intimacy with God. In the early monastic writings, the restoration to paradise was frequently expressed through the monks' closeness to nature and wild beasts. For example, in the story of Abba Amoun, when he is bothered by robbers he summons two large snakes to guard the door of his cell. When the robbers come, they are terrified and rendered insensible by the presence of the snakes:

When Amoun came out he found them [the robbers] unable to speak and almost unconscious. Then raising them up he chided them, 'Do you see how much more ferocious you are than the wild beasts? These, thanks to God, obey our wishes. But you have neither feared God nor respected the piety of Christians.'[14]

Being in God generates peace and right order between Amoun and the serpents. The robbers, because of their sin, do not possess this peace. Sin prevents us from having that basic attitude of listening so that we can hear and follow God's word and obey God's will, manifested in our obligation to love and serve our neighbour.

Intimacy with God was depicted by the transformation of the whole person of the monk shining with radiant glory:

I journeyed on into the desert six or seven miles. I saw a small cave... And I called in front of the cave according to the custom of the brethren, 'Bless me.' Suddenly a great and perfect one of God came out to me, there was a great glory upon his face and his form was very beautiful.[15]

This same splendour is reflected in the face of Antony when he emerges from grappling with the demons in the solitude of the desert.[16] In Chapter 6, we will see this identical radiance in St Dominic de Guzman: a radiance that is an outward manifestation of grace and the life of God within.

It was only after their sin that Adam and Eve perceived they were naked. Their first impulse was to hide themselves from God. They were afraid to be seen, lest the truth of who they were would be revealed. Tragically, they wanted to hide not only from God but also from the truth of their human condition of weakness and need. Their hearts became a closed door, their God-likeness obscured.

We still find ourselves in this condition. Too often, the besetting fear of our culture is the fear to be seen in our vulnerability. So we surround ourselves with things that seem to enhance our image: position, admiration or flatterers, which can be superficial enhancements of our ego. We can build a 'virtual' life. It looks good and exciting, but it is not real. These are the fig leaves we use to try to hide our nakedness. When we hide ourselves from God, we lose the truth of who we are. The men and women of the desert tradition strove for personal integrity before God, without disguise or pretension. The struggle to 'know oneself', grow in self-knowledge and cultivate true self-awareness was central to the spirituality of the desert. 'Above all the Egyptian monks emphasised self-knowledge... they highlight the virtue of discernment, by which they mean an ability to diagnose exactly what is going on at any given moment.'[17]

The monks understood that entering into the depths of their vulnerability and facing honestly their nakedness brought healing and, in due course, security and peace as well. Unmasking their illusions was of great importance. They sought to discern the secret desires and longings of their heart and to bring these desires into conformity with God's desire to heal and restore. It was not introspection: such self-awareness did not come about in a vacuum but in relation to God and God's revealed word in scripture. 'The literary tradition from that world shows them discovering the meaning of the "I" in that question [how can I be saved?] by a genuine awareness of the force of passion within themselves.'[18]

The desert was the place of naked simplicity, a space with a profound capacity for reducing one to the real truths of existence, the truth of oneself and the truth of God. The experiential knowledge of one's own insufficiency and sinfulness, one's inability to attain salvation without grace, gave the monk a heart of compassion for the struggles of others, especially in the light of his own experience of God's forgiving mercy.

We can always be tempted to live on the surface of life. It is safer and less arduous. God desires something more for each of us. Integrity is a mark of holiness. In a person of integrity there is no duplicity between the inner life of mind and heart and the outer life of word and action. The words and actions of the person of holiness reflect the life of the heart. We possess a natural longing for such wholeness, although it can be buried under layers of noise and denial. To enter into this harmony is to become a person of prayer, where worship and life feed and shape one another. Integrity of life is won by the daily choices we make to be honest: people of the word, people to be trusted.

The scriptures were, for these monks, like a mirror reflecting truth. Their continued interaction with the word of God—taking it in, memorising it and allowing it to interact with their thoughts, memories and desires—brought about true self-understanding and conversion. Faithfulness to the power of God's word transformed their minds and hearts.

This lifelong encounter with God's word was part of their asceticism. It was certainly not always easy or seemingly fruitful. Their perseverance at the task of reading, listening and assimilating the word emptied and broke open their hearts for the work of the Holy Spirit. Perseverance remains a vital tool in our spiritual journey. Following Jesus, encountering him in the gospel and allowing the gospel teaching to change them impelled these monks forward to the goal of transformation.

Belonging

In the heart of every man and woman is a deep longing to be loved, to belong. This desire emanates from our innermost spirit where God dwells. It is this inner heart reality that moves us to seek fulfilment and belonging. Paradoxically, the way to find ourselves, our place, our belonging, often begins with separation and leave-taking. Formation in prayer means leave-taking, separating ourselves from those things that pull us away from God. The story of St Antony, often called the father of monasticism, exemplifies this truth.

We can understand Antony's progressive movement from civilisation into the desert as a representation of the inward movement into the innermost centre of his heart, a movement that is necessary for re-creation through grace. Antony's leaving his home, wealth and kindred to begin a life dedicated to God symbolises the movement of God's grace. His story echoes the call of Abraham: 'Go from your country and your kindred and your father's house to the land that I will show you' (Genesis 12:1). God's call is ensconced in the ordinary circumstances of his life: home, church, worship and gospel. Hearing the words of the gospel—'If you wish to be perfect, go, sell your possessions, and give the money to the poor, and you will have treasure in heaven; then come, follow me'

(Matthew 19:21)—empowered Antony to answer God's call to new life circumstances. In their turn, these circumstances would bring about a new movement toward God. Privileged moments of God's grace in the ordinariness of our lives take us by surprise. They impel us toward God in a new way and turn us away from those things that hold us back from growth in God's grace. The beginning point of the journey is the place in which we find ourselves today. Today is always the point of beginning, no matter how far we have travelled.

Antony begins his journey in the town, then moves to the edge of the desert and continues to move farther and farther away from all that he knows, into the very heart of the wilderness. He meets temptations. He grapples with the devil, with his own sins and pain. In the struggle and surrender, he at last finds freedom and home, the place of wholeness and belonging.

The desire for home, belonging, rootedness, springs from the very core of the human heart. It is the belonging and wholeness that arise from our creation in God and for God. To reach this core is to find our place of home, no matter where we reside or what our circumstances are. In the heart's centre we enter into the peace and freedom welling up from God and from what is truest within us.

It was in the heart of the desert, after having lost all that was not God, that Antony found his dwelling place, his home. In God's wonderful providence, at the end of the journey we always find again all that we have lost, but regenerated into our life with God. Antony found God. In finding God, he found himself in a true self-possession, rooted in truth and in the Creator. Antony's story of spiritual struggle in the desert is not accidental but is intimately connected to the transformation of his heart. The desert terrain reflects the wasteland of a heart bereft of God. Movement into the desert coincides with the journey of the heart into wholeness.

Only God can know the fullness of his plan for our life. We only have glimpses and intuitions of the magnificence of his love and plan for us. Each intuition is true, but not yet full enough. Only after we have walked with Jesus through many circumstances can we look back and see the wisdom of his ways and how our lives have grown and become centred. There is something greater, something beyond which we are being called and for which this moment is forming us. Trust is crucial, as is the letting go and going forth that enables God to nurture and deepen the divine mystery of his life within us and for others.

Movement and stability

In the desert tradition there was both movement and stability. In their search for God and for wholeness, these men and women travelled deeper into the desert, yet they also valued the transforming power of remaining in a place. In the tradition, the stable place was the cell, the solitary place where these early monastics would undertake the discipline of seeking God, listening to the word and opening their heart to receive God's grace. We can create stability of place by setting aside moments dedicated to seeking God in the darkness of a quieted and silenced heart. Remaining for the time we have set aside can be an act of fidelity, a commitment beyond the moment of first enthusiasm, even when God seems absent. God is never absent but is always present to us. It is we who need to seek the hidden God of our heart, loving and giving ourselves even in darkness and boredom. We are to stick with the task, not falling into the mindset of seeking instant gratification that is so prevalent in our fluid and fluctuating throwaway society. This practice of abiding and waiting patiently upon God's word propels us forward on our quest for wisdom, oneness and stability.

Is this process of going forth from the known and familiar to the unknown—where even what we think we know, we really do not know at all—possible if we do not literally go into the desert? Of course. Life brings to each of us many desert experiences. How we meet these moments enables us to enter into the process of

transformation. Definitive moments of enlightenment and transformation are enfleshed in the concrete situations of our life. One
such moment, a truly desert experience, could be the death of a
loved one, a serious illness, the end of a relationship, the loss of a
job or the need to move to a new place. Times of upheaval in our
lives are *kairos* moments. (*Kairos* is a Greek word referring not to
chronological time but to a very special time.) These moments call
us forth into another way of being and plunge us into an inward
seeking for meaning and purpose. God uses the circumstances of
our lives to lead us to wisdom.

Unceasing prayer

The term that is used in the desert tradition to describe this creation
of an empty space within is 'purity of heart' or unceasing prayer.
Purity of heart equates with an inner openness, emptiness—a
transparency toward God and the things of God. 'To have a pure
heart is to have a life which wells up in us from a source too deep
for us to plumb. To have a pure heart is to have a heart… which is
constantly being created and sustained by the newness of the life
of God.'[19]

The place of unceasing prayer is the sanctuary of the human
heart, where we meet God. This sacred place within is a place of
silence where we experience God and come to a truer knowledge of
ourselves. This dual knowledge is so important for a life of prayer.
This deep inner space is where we come to our true self and are
united to God.

John Cassian defined unceasing prayer as the grace of continual
prayer found when charity is dwelling in the heart.[20] A divided
heart prays only from time to time. Keeping their gaze fixed upon
God, prayer became for the early monastics a way of life. A heart
given to God prays at all times and in every circumstance. This
is not a prayer of words but of desire and unity. Is this kind of
prayer possible in our busy, activity-orientated world? It seems an

impossible task until we consider unceasing prayer as the direction of the heart toward God.

To pray unceasingly means to form a friendship with God that permeates our whole life and all our actions. Prayer of the heart, this dwelling in our innermost being in love, is not a question of intellectual knowledge, but rather oneness with God and the things of God. It is an awareness of the presence of the Holy Spirit within us, forming us to Jesus and rendering the heart receptive to the movement of grace. 'Lived prayer... to pray without ceasing, that is, to make one's life *into* prayer... That living out, though, is the desert, the *real* desert.[21]

True prayer is never separate from the way we live our lives. The practice of unceasing prayer is developed by a rhythm or discipline of prayer that enters into our hearts and spills over into our lives through our choices and actions. How can this rhythm be applied in our busy schedules? We must create islands of silence in order to slow down, be still and listen to God's word.

Conclusion

The wisdom of the early monastic movement has much to teach us about seeking and surrendering to God. The ascetics' wisdom remains perennial because they were so down-to-earth and sensible in their approach to God, self, and the entire process of conversion and transformation. They did not hide from the truth that would set them free, in a freedom that is so little understood in our society today. The desert Abbas (Fathers) and Ammas (Mothers) had a great respect for the disciplined life and the importance of both perseverance and generosity.

Reflections

On discipline and intentionality

Plan your spiritual day with the same focus and discipline with which you plan your daily work and activities. Designate pockets of prayer throughout the day: for example, the early morning hours, the commute to work, a few moments during the coffee break or lunch hour, queuing at the shops, and in the evening before bed. During these brief moments, direct your inner spirit to God.

5

Of illusion, desire and prayer

For if any are hearers of the word and not doers, they are like those
who look at themselves in a mirror; for they look at themselves and,
on going away, immediately forget what they were like.
JAMES 1:23–24

In his letter to the Romans, Paul speaks of the hold sin has on us.
He writes, 'For I delight in the law of God in my inmost self, but I
see in my members another law at war with the law of my mind,
making me captive to the law of sin that dwells in my members'
(7:22–23). Sin has created division in the human person: a struggle
with the allure of pleasure and gratification to the detriment of our
progress toward what is good and true. The remedy for our divided
condition is Jesus Christ; he is our healing and restoration.

Letting go and opening our spirit to the purifying action of God
is not the task of mystics only; it is the undertaking of all who wish
to follow Christ. We are all called to be mystics, if we understand
this term correctly. The word 'mystical' is not so much about
extraordinary experiences as about entering into the mystery, into
the truth of our destiny, into Jesus. Every person must do this,
sooner or later.

Conversion

In *The Never-ending Story*, Michael Ende's wonderful fantasy book, a little boy named Bastian Balthasar Bux is very unhappy. His father ignores him and his peers make fun of him. He becomes part of 'The Never-ending Story' and enters the land of Fantastica, where he is given a gift of wishes. Wish by wish, he seeks to be transformed, to be powerful, to be handsome, to be loved and to be admired. His wishes all come true, but the change is only on the surface, a veneer. Nothing happens in his heart. Bastian is not really changed; he is merely granted the exterior appearance of all the things he wants to be. 'He had always wanted to be different than he was, but he didn't want to change.'[22] With each new wish, Bastian loses part of his true identity.

This story illustrates well the meaning of 'illusion': we settle for a superficial appearance of being someone or something, without any vital change or growth. In doing so, we bury our God-likeness and replace God with a makeover image to our liking. This behaviour has far-reaching ramifications for how we live, what we consider important and how we communicate with others. Our behaviour also affects the world around us.

Illusions are like masks that cover our true face. They protect us from seeing ourselves as we really are. We can be afraid to confront our weakness and insufficiencies, our poor self-image. A poor self-image is often the result of others imposing expectations on us or of comparing ourselves to others in the light of what the culture considers successful, beautiful and important. God does not view us in this way. God sees us as we really are, in all our beauty and dignity. God loves us with an unconditional love that does not depend on our ability to achieve.

What of the illusions that beset us—our desire for greatness, power, success, adulation and popularity, to name some of the most common? These things are illusory as long as they remain qualities that we acquire without concern for the integrity of our person. We can counteract our illusions by nurturing true self-knowledge. The Desert Fathers and Mothers are a good model. They sought to test, scrutinise and evaluate the myriad conflicting motives arising in their hearts.[23] The great task, as they saw it, was to destroy illusion and deception, and to become persons of integrity. They grappled with their illusions as Jacob grappled with God for his dream for the future (Genesis 32:23–25).

The heart's desire

Human beings are complex, composed of spirit and body. The choices we make that lead to concrete actions in our life are formed by the desires of our heart. What are the desires that motivate us? If we can understand our desires, we can know what things give incentive for our actions. The Abbas and Ammas of the desert considered addressing their inner thoughts as the way to self-honesty. Their intention was to gather their fractured thoughts and desires into singleness of purpose, directed toward leading a focused life. This effort to uncover and give expression to the heart's most urgent longings occupied a central role in the ascetic work of the desert.

How do we discern our thoughts? It is impossible for the mind not to be troubled by all kinds of thoughts and desires, good and bad. The important thing is how we deal with them. It is in our power to sift through our thoughts carefully and decide whether to accept or reject them. To do so presupposes our facility to reflectively shape our existence. What are the character and quality of our thoughts?

Isaiah says of the idols that Israel worshipped, 'They are all a delusion; their works are nothing; their images are empty wind' (Isaiah 41:29). Our illusions can be the false gods we set up to hide from God and to hide from ourselves. We hear the echo of God's question in the garden: 'Where are you?' and Adam's reply, 'I heard the sound of you in the garden, and I was afraid, because

I was naked; and I hid myself' (Genesis 3:9–10).

Our imagination and the content of our memory often fill our inner quietude with a cacophony of sound. The memory's temptations are many: the inability to forgive past hurts and to move on, or the memory of the pleasure of past sins. What fills our memory is important because, in the quietness of prayer, its content will surface. To hear God's word clearly, the babble of thoughts within must cease so that we can create a quiet place for God to speak. Part of learning to be empty is to learn what fills us. The desert dwellers believed that attention to our impulses helps us to understand what motivates our actions. They revealed their thoughts to the Elder, a man or woman of experience and wisdom, in their search for radical honesty. A good spiritual director could be a guide as we seek the truth of who we are and understand the desires that possess us. Mindfulness of our thoughts fosters growth in our ability to perceive the truth about ourselves, about God, and about the world.

Emptiness

For the Desert Mothers and Fathers, the desert was the place to leave behind the superficial and return to the essential, to find again the one thing necessary. The emptiness and sameness of the desert terrain reflects the journey of going out from our known thoughts and desires into God's desire for us.

Today, we must use the events of our lives for the desert moments of emptying. The emptying process begins when we seek God's will in our daily life. To enlarge our capacity for life, for wisdom, truth and love, emptying is a prerequisite. The process of emptying forms a heart-space that no longer obscures what is true and beautiful. Emptiness of our own way of seeing gives us new eyes to see the wonder of God's vision. Our emptiness of driven desires creates a space for God to fill us with love and expands our capacity for living fully. We can then be reformed to God's dream for us, which we received at our creation.

I went down to the potter's house and there he was, working at the wheel. Whenever the object of clay which he was making turned out badly in his hand, he tried again, making of the clay another object of whatever sort he pleased. 'Then the word of the Lord came to me: 'Can I not do to you… as the potter has done?' (Jeremiah 18:3–6)

Reflections

Discerning the motives of the heart

Do a daily examination of conscience. Instead of just compiling a list of faults, centre your intention inward. Look with radical self-honesty at your fears, your defensiveness, your relationship with others, and the ways you have or have not sought relationship with God. You can discern your inner spirit by looking at the desires that move you. Write down these insights.

Our reactions to people and situations can tell us much more about ourselves than about the other. Question your reactions.

6

St Dominic: icon of prayer and action

I do not cease to give thanks for you as I remember you in my prayers… so that, with the eyes of your heart enlightened, you may know what is the hope to which he has called you.
EPHESIANS 1:16, 18

St Dominic de Guzman was born in the Castilian village of Caleruega, around the year 1171. A man of prayer and study who was known for his great compassion and joy, he studied at the University of Palencia before joining the canons regular of Osma around 1196. In 1203 he accompanied the bishop, Diego, on a royal mission through France. This missionary journey exposed Dominic to the problems the church faced with the Albigensian heretics. He founded the Order of Friars Preachers to make known the message of the gospel and the name of the Lord Jesus Christ throughout the world. The Order received from the church the mandate to preach. Dominic desired the preaching of the Order to be rooted firmly in the study of scripture and theology. He died on 6 August 1221, in Bologna.

The saints are icons of holiness 'written' by the Holy Spirit. An icon is not simply a painting, but an image that is meant to draw us into the mystery of God, the saving mystery mediated through Jesus. These holy men and women reproduce Christ in their lives, thus teaching us what it means truly to follow Jesus and do his works in the world. They are the face of Christ for a specific historical moment and beyond that moment as a living gospel for future generations. Dominic is certainly such an icon of Jesus Christ, the Word of God, and of gospel living.

In Chapter 3, we called Catherine of Siena an iconographer of prayer because she wrote of the spiritual journey using word images that deepen our understanding of God. We speak of Dominic as an icon of prayer because his teaching is received through the example of his life rather than through his writing. Dominic was not a writer; he was a man of action—action that flowed from a profound union with God through Jesus Christ. In his vocation, Dominic replicated the mission of the Word made flesh, sent forth from the Father into the world for our salvation, and the mission of the church to preach the good news of salvation. Dominic's life exemplifies the dynamism that comes from being one with God. This man of God is a paradigm of the person of integrity whose action flows from contemplation, one in whom there was no duplicity between the impetus of the heart and action.

One of the defining characteristics of Dominic's call to holiness is intercession for the salvation of all people. We will explore this characteristic of Dominic as a lesson that we can apply to our own spiritual journey. How does interceding for others fit into the theme of this book on the human person as the place of prayer? Can intercessory prayer be contemplative, radiating from our innermost heart as a source of God's saving grace for others? Yes. We can become a place of prayer for others because we have entered into God. The human person is the place of God's dwelling and thus the place of God's salvation in this moment of history. St Dominic is an example of such a place of prayer for others, through his life and through the Order he founded. Let us begin by considering Dominic the man of prayer, formed by the word of God. We will then examine Dominic as an icon of prayer for others.

Formed by the word of God

Dominic was formed by constant reflection on the scriptures. He carried the Gospel of Matthew and letters of Paul with him on his preaching journeys, at all times savouring the word of God.[24] He broke open the word and studied with 'continual eagerness, to drink from the streams of Sacred Scripture'.[25] His study reverberated in his innermost being and prepared him, like Antony of the desert, for his future call as founder and preacher.

He was a doer of the word for God's glory and the salvation of all. Hearing the word is insufficient if it does not then enter the heart and transform us. To hear carries the connotation of completion in transformation. The word of God is not a book one reads; it is active and alive, transforming mind and heart. Hearing the word is a process.

'There are two ways of keeping God's word, namely, one whereby we store in our memory whatever we hear, and the other whereby we put into practice what we have heard.'[26] Dominic did both. God's word fell on the fertile soil of his heart and bore fruit a hundredfold (see Matthew 13:1–23). A life of virtue produces the good soil that enables the word to grow and ripen through the ongoing process of spiritual maturing. Being a doer of the word establishes us in a rhythm of prayer.

'Other seeds fell on rocky ground, where they did not have much soil, and they sprang up quickly, since they had no depth of soil. But when the sun rose, they were scorched; and since they had no root, they withered away' (Matthew 13:5–6). Depth of soil means allowing the seed to fall into our innermost heart. We prepare the good soil by our receptivity to the seed of God's word. Dominic must have frequently pondered this passage and sensed his call to sow God's word, first in his own heart, then beyond himself, in the hearts of all God's children. The mysterious impulses of the Holy Spirit shape us to the realisation of our vocation. A word, a circumstance, a longing desire: these indicate God's will for us. As we follow these intuitions, the Holy Spirit confirms the rightness of our choices. In the case of Dominic, his meditations on the Gospel of Matthew, the impulses of his heart and the circumstances of his life drew him into God's plan.

This man of God was obedient to the inner prompting of the Holy Spirit. Someone who listened attentively to the word, he was impelled forward in his ministry by the word he heard. The gospel, for Dominic, was the book of life. He was a missionary. His task was to bring salvation to all through proclaiming the good news. Dominic's appropriation of the scriptures defined his mission and separated him from all that was not God's will for him.

Dominic's life is a teaching on being an active participant in the grace of Christ, on being a person whose life is focused on the task of holiness and who seeks with intensity the purpose of God.

The words he preached reflected the dispositions of his heart. It is abundantly clear by what was written of Dominic's holiness, transparency and immense liberty that he had attained purity of heart. He was a man of freedom because he possessed a listening heart. His obedient freedom found its source in his love for Jesus Christ—a love that informed all he did and enabled him to embrace the future, the present task and whatever challenges came his way.

Grace formed Dominic to be who he was for others, to accomplish the truly great tasks of founding the Order of Preachers, tireless preaching, night prayer and miracles. And so it is with each of us. Dominic did the works of Jesus, just as Jesus stated in the Gospel. Jesus promised that we would do even greater works than he through the Spirit (John 14:12), an amazing assurance that we need to take seriously. We are called to be God's presence in the world, and we can fulfil that mission through our obedient listening and openness to being formed by the gospel.

Dominic stood before God in every situation, attuned to God's will. Just as is the case for each of us, seeking God's will was a gradual process informed by the circumstances of his life, including his weaknesses. In being faithful to the various moments of grace,

Dominic became an instrument of God's grace. He was a man of unceasing prayer. The diverse elements that made up his day found their unity in his union with God. His prayer was an almost unbroken conversation with our Lord Jesus Christ: 'It was his custom to spend his night-watches in prayer and, having shut the door, to pray to the Father in secret… His frequent and special prayer to God was for the gift of true charity capable of labouring for and procuring the salvation of [all].'[27]

A contemplative by night, he was an apostle during the day. We are told that his countenance was always open and joyful; he was a man wholly turned outward to others: 'The one passion of his life was to preach a truth he could not keep to himself. And he preached it by word and by example. But also—to a remarkable degree—he preached it by joy.'[28]

His wisdom and vision came from the purity of his heart in tune with God's word. This receptivity to the work of the Holy Spirit helped him to understand the deep truths of the faith and to teach them with clarity to others. Dominic penetrated difficult questions 'through the humble understanding of his heart'.[29]

Intercession for others

People saw that Dominic was one whose heart had achieved total transparency to others through the love of God fully possessing his heart. Such transparency is not possible without self-denial. The actions of this gracious preacher proceeded from his heart's core. Thus, Dominic is an icon of the human person as the place of prayer from which loving service to his sisters and brothers emanates. His inwardness strengthened him to go forth continually in love to his neighbour with an untiring zeal that is possible only through God's grace. His very person radiated the presence of God. 'From his brow and eyes emanated a kind of radiance which drew everyone to revere and love him. Dominic was genial in his relationship with others. He was pleasant and affable. He was friendly to all, peaceable.'[30] Joy, radiance and peace overflowing in goodness and love are certainly gospel characteristics and a sign of the work of the Holy Spirit.

The letter to the Hebrews tells us that Jesus stands before the Father, forever making intercession for us (7:25). The prayer of intercession flowing from a life united to God is a contemplative experience and a realised union with the prayer of Jesus, particularly the prayer of Jesus upon the cross. Thus, when we speak of Dominic as an icon of intercession for others, we mean that because he was one with the redemptive will of Christ, his life and actions were dedicated to mediation for others. Those who knew Dominic always spoke of his cry during the night hours of prayer: 'What will become of sinners?'

Dominic entered into Jesus' prayer of intercession. By being one with the mind of Christ and God's will to save, we too will become the place of intercession for all people. Entering into the redemptive prayer of Jesus encompasses not only our words but the whole experience of our lives. The Gospels are clear: we cannot truly love God without loving our neighbour. The two loves exist and grow together.

Dominic's holiness is inseparable from his mission. Dominican scholar Simon Tugwell writes, 'What we know of the prayer of St Dominic shows that it was habitually intercessory.'[31] The foundation of the Order of Preachers, an Order dedicated to preaching the name of the Lord Jesus, is a work of grace that flowed from Dominic's presence to God. Dominic sought God through a life of prayer, which was poured out in love for his neighbour. He was a contemplative who was known for his equilibrium, for his peacefulness of spirit and compassion—a man deeply in love with Jesus Christ. Because he was totally united to Jesus, he was a man for others. A man of vision who learned wisdom in contemplation of the crucified, he is often depicted in meditation at the foot of the cross. Dominic loved and followed Jesus with such an ardent heart that he was on fire with love for all God's people. In a vision,

Catherine of Siena saw Dominic's close connection to the mission of Christ as coming forth from the Father: 'She saw the Son of God coming forth from the mouth of the Eternal Father. And then, to her amazement, she saw, emerging from the Father's breast, "the most blessed Patriarch Dominic".'[32]

Who Dominic was and how he lived illustrate prayer as flowing from a relationship with God—a relationship of love and service that moves into God and then proceeds outward in love for our sisters and brothers.

Conclusion

In our spiritual journey, we do not reproduce exactly the life of any saint; each person is called to reflect Jesus Christ in a unique manner. Dominic's life is like a road map with certain signposts along the way that can give clearer instructions on the road to follow, the way of Christ. Jordan of Saxony wisely writes:

Who would be able to imitate perfectly the virtue of this man? We can but admire his example and permit it to show us the inertia of our own times. But for anyone else to be able to accomplish what he accomplished would be a work, not of human power, but of a special grace of God's merciful goodness calling one to a like degree of holiness.[33]

What Dominic accomplished, as Jordan writes, was not the result of human power but a sharing in God's grace; his energy and effectiveness came from God. Paul writes to the Ephesians that to each of us a grace is given in Christ (4:7). Jesus promises that even in the midst of our weakness, God's power at work in us is sufficient and made clearly known in weakness (2 Corinthians 12:9). St Dominic is, for us, a model of what God's grace can do in someone who is receptive to the work of the Holy Spirit. The same Holy Spirit will work in each of us, perfecting us in our particular vocation and the way we are called to be the Christ presence to those around us.

Reflections

On intercession

Before praying for others, take time to centre yourself in God. Ask God what his plan is for this person. Ask how you need to intercede for this person, and then begin your prayer of intercession, asking the Holy Spirit for guidance. Carry the needs of your family, friends and all who cross your path in your heart and in God's love.

7

Etty Hillesum: the inner room

We must forget all our big words, begin with God and end with death, and we must become as simple as spring water. [34]

Etty Hillesum was born on 15 January 1914, into a Jewish family. They were living in Holland during World War II as Hitler began to exterminate the Jews. In 1942 Etty went voluntarily to Westerbork, a transit camp for Jews in the eastern part of the Netherlands, near the German border. She stayed for only a few weeks because of illness. She returned to the camp a few months later to accompany her people and do what little she could to ease their situation. The camp was the last stop before Auschwitz for more than 100,000 Jews. The conditions in the camp steadily worsened as the round-up and deportation of Jews escalated. Her father, mother and brother Mischa joined her later. All four were transported to Auschwitz in September 1943, and all four perished there. Etty died on 30 November 1943. She had given her journals to Maria Tuinzing, a friend, to pass on to Klaas Smelik, the only writer Etty knew. She wanted Smelik to see that they were eventually published. He was unable to do so, but his son published the diaries about 40 years after her death.

A unique witness

Etty is a contemplative and an exemplar for the human person as the sacred place of prayer. What we know of her comes from her journals, her letters to family and friends and their letters to her, along with testimonies from those who knew her. Her journals reveal Etty's search for personal healing and human integration, along with her search for God. She began the journals on 8 March 1941, when she was 27 years old; the last journal entry that we have was written on 13 October 1942. The extant letters date from 1941 to 1943, ending with a postcard that she threw from the train on her way to Auschwitz in September 1943. Her writings span just two short years, but how much happened in those years! What a tremendous amount of transformation fills the journals and is reflected in the letters.

Etty is very much a woman of our time, a person intently seeking God and human wholeness in a world shaped by Godless philosophies and a lack of value for the human person. Etty, although a Jew by birth, knew nothing about the Jewish faith. What is especially amazing about Etty is that the work of the Holy Spirit began in her while she was still unconnected to any particular religious formation and was very much a woman who was immersed in the cultural standards of her day. Yet her experience of the God within stands in a long tradition of God-seekers.

It was not until she met Julius Spier, a Jungian psychoanalyst, that Etty began a serious reflection on the Bible, including the New Testament. Julius Spier, who was also Jewish, introduced her not only to the New Testament but to other Christian literature as well. She frequently read Augustine's *Confessions* and, in the last year of her life, she read a great deal of Meister Eckhart, a Dominican mystic of the Rhineland. It was Spier who suggested that Etty begin keeping a diary, probably as a part of her therapy (*Etty*, p. xiii). During this period she assimilated the gospel teaching and the words of Jesus, which are not only quoted throughout the journals but are also put into practice.

Etty's response to the Nazis is surprising. It is the response of one who sees things from God's perspective. She believed that people were to do what they could to make the world better, but, in the end, it was not in doing but in being the transformed receptacle of God's presence in the world that she would transform her moment in history. 'This is something people refuse to admit to themselves: at a given point you can no longer *do*, but can only be and accept' (*Etty*, p. 628).

What answer did Etty find in this dark time in history? The only answer possible: love and forgiveness. In her search for human truth and wholeness in the midst of the chaotic, violent and irrational treatment of the Jewish people, she came to understand and assimilate the gospel teaching of love. She had a profound spiritual sense of her connectedness not only with this epoch of history but with every age and all human persons. Such a connectedness can only be experienced fully through union with the God of history and eternity: 'A hint of eternity steals through my smallest daily activities and perceptions. I am not alone in my tiredness or sickness or fears, but at one with millions of others from many centuries, and it is all part of life' (*Etty*, p. 466).

The early journals are a constant dialogue with herself as she confronts her shifting emotions and struggles with depression. We find a real growth in Etty as her journal progresses, as she moves into an honest self-awareness, which at last blossoms into contemplative awareness, integrity in her person, peace and joy in all the circumstances of life. Etty was not perfect. She lived a bohemian and free lifestyle. Her writings do not record an instant conversion to a new way of life. Rather, God's grace works in her gradually and through the imperfect circumstances of her life. This in itself is a great testimony to God's loving kindness and infinite mercy, and encouragement for all of us who give ourselves to God. Etty writes, 'It is a slow and painful process, this striving after true freedom' (*Etty*, p. 134).

Like the early monastics, she looks at the motives and needs that animate her interactions with others, and thus comes to a deeper self-understanding. It is God who brings Etty into the peace that surpasses understanding; at the same time, her discipline and seeking open her heart to God's grace. Here we have the great paradox of growth in contemplation: all is grace, yet our work of emptying is also an important part of the process. God is always willing to inundate us with the abundance of his grace, but never violates our free will to choose.

This effort to be free was a springboard for Etty's growth in love. She realised that her vocation was not in loving or giving herself totally to one person, but rather in opening her heart to everyone. She discovered over time that true freedom is attained only when we can be comfortable with our own solitude, our own uniqueness.

I believe this is what Etty means when she writes, 'I know two sorts of loneliness.' She describes the first as disconnectedness from others, herself and the purpose of life, a loneliness created by alienation from reality; the second is connectedness to reality and to herself, a possession of herself in unity with others but not dependent on them. What she is talking about in the second case I equate with the inner solitude of one who has come to true knowledge of herself and of God. She writes of this loneliness, 'Life may be brimming over with experiences, but somewhere, deep inside, all of us carry a vast and fruitful loneliness wherever we go' (*Etty*, p. 305).

Etty longs for her emotions to become more integrated and at the service of her whole person. All this longing is resolved in her journals, which move from an intense introspection to knowing herself and knowing all reality through the prism of the God within.

She sought the simplicity that unites and gives harmony to the complex situations and relationships of life. Inner unity is a gift each of us can possess; with this gift, life becomes very different—

not in itself, but because of our attitudes and perceptions. In a practical way, life in Jesus changes everything and brings stability and happiness, as God has promised.

Transformation: vocation to love

Etty's growth in simplicity and truth produced at the same time a greater ability to expand her heart in love for others. She was deeply grateful to God for the overwhelming love that filled her: 'To think that one small human heart can experience so much, oh God, so much suffering and so much love, I am so grateful to You, God, for having chosen my heart in these times... I love people so terribly, because in every human being I love something of You' (*Etty*, p. 514).

Her spiritual growth becomes almost palpable in her middle journals. She linked her interior discipline with an understanding that the task she was undertaking had real ramifications for her neighbour and the world about her. Her inner listening was no longer only to herself but was also to others and to their needs. Others must find a place in the sanctuary of her heart. She found herself incapable of hatred, even of the most vicious of Nazi soldiers. She writes, 'We must help to increase the store of love in this world. Every bit of hate we add to the surfeit of hate there already is, renders this world more inhospitable and inhabitable' (*Etty*, p. 471).

She knew that whatever evil could be found in others could also be found in herself—another repeated theme as the journals evolve. Here we have the example of compassion learned by those who have sincerely faced their own fragility, weakness and sin. When we know experientially our own need for mercy, we can extend mercy to others. This is part of becoming like God and being recreated in God's image. 'The rottenness of others is in us, too... I really see no other solution than to turn inward and to root out all the rottenness there. I no longer believe that we can change anything in the world until we have first changed ourselves' (*Etty*, p. 245).

Her belief that we can change nothing in the world until we have first changed ourselves is a recurring aspect of Etty's mysticism. Truly it would be a better world if we spent as much energy naming our own weakness, and seeking and praying to change, as we put forth criticising and trying to remake others, which is a task that only God can accomplish. If we were each at peace with the unique person we are, not desiring to be what others are or to have what others possess, then there would be no greed, no hatred or war.

This is a powerful commentary on our responsibility to love. It matters to the whole world if I do not love, if I do not bring peace to my surroundings. This is the primary responsibility of being Christian. Etty understood that the evil in the world comes not from God but from us.

Yet Etty did not feel powerless in the face of persecution and the pain of being a Jew at this time in Holland. Her sense of power came from within. The true source of peace is the peace abiding in each human person.

I find life beautiful and I feel free. The sky within me is as wide as the one stretching above my head. I believe in God and I believe in man, and I say so without embarrassment. True peace will come only when every individual finds peace within himself; when we have all vanquished and transformed our hatred for our fellow human beings of whatever race— even into love one day, although perhaps that is asking too much. It is, however the only solution. (Etty, pp. 434–435)

Faith in God strengthened her, sustaining her in suffering but also infusing the senseless suffering of her people with beauty and love for life.

Integrity and synthesis

With spiritual maturity came a new synthesis of motivation and action for which Etty had so often prayed and longed: 'Oh, Lord, let me feel at one with myself. Let me perform a thousand daily tasks with love, but let every one spring from a greater central core of devotion and love. Then it won't really matter what I do and where I am' (*Etty*, p. 165).

In God she participated in an eternal now of peace and integrity: joy, suffering and love were fused in a new possession of oneness. In her new way of being in God, she finds herself joyfully divested of her wishes and desires:

It is as if I shed further burdens from moment to moment, as if all the divisions there now are between men and nations are being removed for me. There are moments when I can see right through life and the human heart, when I understand more and more and become calmer and calmer and am filled with a faith in God that has grown so quickly inside me that it frightened me at first but has now become inseparable from me. (Etty, p. 481)

She recognises that suffering is part of life. She does not love suffering or pain or think one should seek suffering, but she knows that one must bear with love and dignity the suffering that life brings unbidden. What matters is to cope with what comes but to 'keep a small corner of one's soul unsullied, come what may' (*Etty*, p. 483).

Mystical sense of suffering

As her inward perception grew and she grasped more fully a purpose and meaning in her life, suffering and a sense of oneness with other human beings took root. She understood that her life and her suffering were linked in some way to this moment of history and to the suffering of all the Jews: 'I feel like a small battle field, in which the problems, or some of the problems, of our time are being fought out. All one can hope to do is to keep oneself humbly available, to allow oneself to be a battlefield' (*Etty*, p. 63).

Etty is not willing to save herself. She refuses to do anything that would exempt her from sharing the lot of her people. It is a clear decision on her part: she fully recognises the reality of what is happening to the Jews and what the consequences of her actions will be: 'And if I should not survive, how I die will show me who I really am' (*Etty*, p. 487). Her friends wanted her to save herself but Etty could not choose to do so at the expense of someone else. She had a deep sense of her freedom in God and in her peaceful possession of herself.

They say everyone who can must try to stay out of their clutches… And the funny thing is I don't feel I'm in their clutches anyway, whether I stay or am sent away… I don't feel in anybody's clutches; I feel safe in God's arms… I may face cruelty and deprivation the likes of which I cannot imagine in even my wildest fantasies. Yet all this is as nothing to the immeasurable expanse of my faith in God and my inner receptiveness. (Etty, p. 487)

Etty knew that there was nothing that could stop the terrible violence and persecution perpetrated against her people. The source of this wrongdoing did not rest in God but in the unconverted hearts of women and men. Her faith in God never wavered; she freely chose to share the lot of so many others. She also had great confidence that God could use her, whatever the circumstances of her life.

Helping God

In the journals, Etty uses an interesting and at first shocking phrase in describing her mission. The phrase is a hallmark of her spirituality and a decisive image of the freedom God gives to his children to make choices, whether good or destructive. She writes, 'But one thing is becoming increasingly clear to me: *that You cannot help us, that we must help You to help ourselves…* all that really matters: that we safeguard that little piece of You, God, in ourselves. And perhaps in others as well' (*Etty*, p. 488, author's emphasis).

Etty does not hold God responsible because she believes that the hatred, violence and cruelty are not God's will but the will of his creatures. If goodness and love are to conquer hatred, then it will be through the love carried in the hearts of those who know God and love others with God's love.

The place of God's dwelling

Etty was the place of God's dwelling. In that secret place, God was present not only to her but in the midst of the world and all the chaos of this moment of history through her. She brought God to Westerbork, to her suffering people, radiating God's love, concern and peace through her loving and cheerful service: the gift of herself to others. Because God was in Etty, the whole world was a better world. Redemption and beauty were brought to so much cruelty. This is the gift, the real gift of a mystic—to be God's presence in the world. She had a great longing to be an instrument in helping the God-life to grow in others. Etty believed so completely that carrying God, abiding in the God who dwelt in her, was the meaning of all meanings. The door of the intimate room of her heart was thrown wide open to make a home for all humanity.

Westerbork: the final journey

How she lived at Westerbork and how she left on the train speak volumes about Etty. She never lost sight of God's beauty in every moment of her life, and her love for her neighbour continued to grow:

You have made me so rich, oh God, please let me share out Your beauty with open hands. My life has become an uninterrupted dialogue with You, O God, one great dialogue. Sometimes when I stand in some corner of the camp, my feet planted on Your earth, my eyes raised toward your heaven, tears sometimes run down my face, tears of deep gratitude. At night, too, when I lie in my bed and rest in You, oh God, tears of gratitude run down my face, and that is my prayer. (Etty, p. 640)

She protected her mother, father and brother as long as she could from transport, but soon it was impossible to do anything more. A universal love is reflected in her journal entry on the Gospel text of Luke 14:26, about not loving mother or father or even one's life above God: 'More and more I tend toward the idea that love for everyone who may cross your path, love for everyone made in God's image, must rise above love for blood relatives' (*Etty*, p. 641). She wanted to take everything to herself, into her inner sanctuary, not running from any of the reality she was experiencing. Her last extant journal ends with these words: 'We should be willing to act as a balm for all wounds' (*Etty*, p. 550).

Her final letters from Westerbork to friends are beautiful and heart-rending. In one, she describes the weekly transport to Poland where the elderly, the sick and even unaccompanied babies and small children are loaded on the train in order to make up the required quota. Even though transport nights are, as Etty writes, like being in hell (*Etty*, p. 646), she still finds the beauty of a rainbow over the camp (*Etty*, p. 631). And God is always there with Etty, the God of love and hope:

I always end up with just one single word: God. And that says every-thing, and there is no need for anything more. And all my creative powers are translated into inner dialogues with You. The beat of my heart has grown deeper, more active and yet more peaceful, and it is as if I were all the time storing up inner riches. (Etty, p. 640)

Then, suddenly, the time comes. Her whole family is put on the transport train to Auschwitz. The last communication from Etty, a postcard she throws from the train, is picked up by a farmer and posted.

Christine, opening the Bible at random I find this: 'The Lord is my high tower.' I am sitting on my rucksack in the middle of a full freight car. Father, Mother, and Mischa are a few cars away. In the end, the departure came without warning... We left the camp singing, Father and Mother firmly and calmly, Mischa too. We shall be travelling for three days. Thank you for all your kindness and care. (Etty, pp. 658–659)

Conclusion

From Etty we can learn many things. We learn of the interior room that every person carries within, that hidden room where God abides and where we enter into God's presence. Those who find that room within find God, and also their true self, their vocation and the truth of their existence.

Etty Hillesum continues to be a gift—to our generation and every generation—of the beautiful mystery of the indwelling God, a union that is salvific, not only for ourselves but for all God's children. Etty is an excellent model for those who live the contemplative life because she lived so fully the contemplative reality of being in God as the source of salvation and life. Etty knew she was called primarily to 'be', to be the place that holds salvation because she was God's temple. Her life stands as an example not only for those who have chosen to live a life withdrawn in prayer but also for every person who wants to live as God's presence in the midst of the world. How we are called to live this mystery will be made manifest in our particular life through the Holy Spirit.

God calls us to the full reality of our creation, our re-creation in Christ; we enter the journey to wholeness one step at a time. Etty was chosen when she did not know God and while she was yet very wounded. God's choice does not depend on our goodness, our beauty, our wealth or our abilities, but on our being the unique person we are, created in God's image. Listening to life, to our circumstances, to our heart in truth will reveal the still, small voice of the Holy Spirit whispering from moment to moment the way to God, to re-creation and wholeness in Jesus.

A letter from one of Etty's companions in Westerbork, describing how she went to the train that transported her to Auschwitz, sums up Etty so well:

Talking gaily, smiling, a kind word for everyone she met on the way, full of sparkling good humour, perhaps just a touch of sadness, but every inch our Etty, the way you all know her... she herself is going on and on towards the East, where she so wanted to go. I think she was actually quite looking forward to this experience, to sharing anything and everything in store for us all... And the way [the inmates] felt about her leaving spoke volumes for the love and dedication she had given them all. (Etty, pp. 667–668)

Reflections

On dwelling in the inner room of the heart
Set aside a period of silence, about ten minutes each day (increase the time when and if you are able). Look inward. Think of a small, still point within yourself, deeper than the many thoughts that may bombard you in the silence. Do not address these thoughts, but see yourself sinking deeper to the still point of light within. You can repeat an inner phrase or word of scripture, but do not even focus on that; just allow it to repeat itself within you as you seek the deep point of silence within.

Listen to the God who speaks and to the whispering of your heart. In the silence you will learn to hear the inner voice of the Holy Spirit and the deepest longings of your heart.

8

Finding our centre

'Peace I leave with you; my peace I give to you. I do not give to you as the world gives. Do not let your hearts be troubled, and do not let them be afraid.'
JOHN 14:27

A family usually has one special room where everyone gathers to be together. One could say that this is the centre of the home. We each have such a room in our heart's core, where we meet God. Our innermost centre is where we are rooted; the place of our true home, the centre of our belonging and the sacred place of prayer. This is where we worship in spirit and truth, as Jesus told the Samaritan woman: 'The hour is coming, and is now here, when the true worshippers will worship the Father in spirit and truth' (John 4:23).

How do we learn to dwell in the sacred space of the heart? Finding our centre cannot be an impossible task. God desires to dwell with us and wants us to find our place of unity and wholeness. How, then, do we enter this sanctuary? It is as simple as opening the door and crossing the threshold of not one but many doors that the circumstances and events in our life provide.

A door is a multi-layered image. We can picture the doors as progressive; crossing the threshold of one door brings us further into the mystery of our self and leads us to other doors that must be opened at God's right time. Entering our heart chamber is never separate from the everyday events of our lives. The door is a symbol of crisis moments, changing circumstances and other such times when we know our life is changing and new challenges present themselves. Each door has similar characteristics. It is a closed door through which we feel called to enter, although we do not know what lies on the other side. God invites us to open the door but does not reveal what awaits us. We must step through into the unknown, into the darkness; our only guarantee is trust in the God who calls us.

A dear friend of mine, Beth, once shared with me a recurring dream she experienced. She dreamed about a walk-in closet in her bedroom that was not only closed but pegged shut. That closet terrified her. She longed for freedom from her fear and a new way of being, and desired to give herself to God and to follow Jesus. This longing was the light of the Holy Spirit at work in her. The dream held the secret to her need for healing and God's desire to heal. As she opened her heart to the presence of the Holy Spirit, the dream began to change. In her dream she was no longer afraid of the closet and wanted to throw open the door and enter it. As this desire increased, my friend dreamed that she took out all the pegs, threw open the door and entered into the dark space within. It was full of ghosts that she could neither see nor dispel, but she was no longer afraid. She woke up that night saying, 'In the name of the Lord Jesus, come out.'

She shared her dream with her spiritual director, who knew her personal story. Beth came from an abusive home and thought, perhaps, this closet of ghosts was some repressed memory of her home life. In their discussion, he suggested that the closet was not filled with something bad or evil; rather, it was the chamber of her deepest self and all those true parts of herself she had buried behind the closed door of her inner sanctuary in order to survive her loveless growing-up years. Beth sensed that this was the true interpretation of her dream; in fact, the dream never recurred afterwards. For Beth, this was one of the doors that needed to be opened for her healing and transformation. God's way for her from that time on became a movement out of fear and into vulnerability. Step by step, she had the courage to face her own woundedness, to reveal herself and to allow others to come to know her.

A passage from fear is always a movement into trust. Such a passage is certainly not without pain and at times involves intense hurt. Beth walked in the light of the gentle and loving revelation of the Holy Spirit, who formed her to Jesus. She could do it only with the sustaining presence of God's strength, with faith in God's love for her, and with the help of wise and spiritual brothers and sisters. We, too, can find the strength in God to travel through what holds us in bondage.

Are we willing to open the door? Opening the door is synonymous with the journey toward knowledge of God and a true knowledge of self. Coming to know ourselves without pretence or masks can be a fearsome task, but these pretences are the closed doors that do not allow us to enter into the hidden sanctuary of the heart. What carries us over the threshold is the willingness to see ourselves in our nakedness and not be ashamed, the strength to be uncomfortable with our way of thinking and doing, and the courage to enter into a new space. This is the formula for finding our inner room, entering it and making our innermost centre the place of our dwelling. Catherine of Siena's teaching on the cell of self-knowledge can help us to understand what this room is and how we are transformed by entering into it.

The cell of self-knowledge

The cell (or room) of self-knowledge is the place of communication between the soul and God—the empty (and emptied) space within the human person where one can listen to God. Catherine's cell of self-knowledge is the place of the heart where God dwells, the place where we enter into the 'sea of peace' who is the Trinity. Catherine writes:

In this cell you will find God. For just as God holds within himself everything that shares in being, so you will find within yourself memory, which holds, and is well-suited to hold, the treasure of God's blessing. There too you will find understanding, which makes us sharers in the wisdom of God's Son by understanding and knowing his will, a will that wants nothing but that we be made holy. You will also find there the gentle mercy of the Holy Spirit, the aspect of God that gives and is nothing but love.[35]

Home and place of belonging

Catherine likens this inner cell to a house. It is the home where we dwell with God in intimacy and love. She often wrote to her disciples of her longing that they make their permanent home in the cell of self-knowledge, for it is there that we find the secret of love and loving. There we understand ourselves in relation to God, who has created us. In this cell, 'We see our own nothingness, that our very existence is ours by grace and not because we have a right to it, and every grace beyond our existence as well—it is all given to us with boundless love.'[36]

What Catherine means by 'seeing our own nothingness' is not something negative but the truth that our being has been created out of God. We are 'nothing' because all that we are is a received reality. This is a tremendous and supremely comforting insight. Catherine goes on to say that once we have found the God-life within us, we seek to find God everywhere, in all the circumstances of our life and in our neighbour. Because we have found the indwelling presence of God in our heart, we recognise God's presence and providence everywhere.

The secret chamber of the heart is a place where we remain in union with God. It is a cell of solitude, a place of peace, truth and oneness. This room within is a place of wholeness that equips us for loving service to our sisters and brothers. It is a permanent dwelling in the midst of life's activity.

What is this two-chambered cell that Catherine is speaking of? It is the cell of knowledge of God and knowledge of the self. The cell is the core of our being where we reflect God and where the truth of who we are is one with the truth of who God is, different as image and reality, but nevertheless one in the unity of reflected truth. This cell is the place of unity where we are restored to the creative image that was ours in the beginning.

Self-knowledge and truth

Catherine, throughout her teaching, equates true knowledge of self, grasped in the house of self-knowledge, with humility. In this house we grow in a profound knowledge of ourselves in the light of the Holy Spirit, who is the fire of God's love. The fire of the Spirit purifies and transforms us, strengthens and comforts us. We come to know the truth of our poverty through the illumination of the Holy Spirit in such a way that it liberates our spirit and fills us with joy. The cell of self-knowledge becomes a garden where we are no longer afraid or ashamed to walk with God. This dual knowledge is the source of peace. With delightful insight Catherine says that self-knowledge helps us 'so that we don't get things out of perspective when we are happy or become impatient when we are sad'.[37]

Self-knowledge and prayer

Those who have come to dwell in their heart 'find prayer everywhere, because they always carry with them the place where God dwells by grace and where we ought to pray': the sacred place of prayer.[38] It is here in our true home that desire becomes unceasing prayer. Here we enter into God's eternal heart, into the womb of God, and are reborn clothed with the fiery love of the triune God.

The frantic pace and noise of our world have drawn many people further away from the quiet listening that is needed to journey to our inner still point. All of us, at times, even in the midst of almost insurmountable distractions, experience a hidden longing for peace, for wholeness. This is our heart's call to prayer and communion. In order to begin the journey, we need to surrender our fear, and walk trusting in God's love and the divine plan for our life.

True solitude

Solitude is not isolationism, a nice comfortable world of escape that we create for ourselves. True solitude is a place of confrontation, of struggle, of encounter and, finally, of transformation. To see ourselves in our uniqueness is to experience solitude. Because each of us is unique, an individual, we already know what it means to be solitary. We are alone in the sense that we are not the other. We need to face and live the truth of our unique existence. Real holiness is wedded to authentic human life, and therefore to our individuality, our talents, our potential, our limitations and our weaknesses.

It is only in opening every hidden corner of our being before God that we are made whole. This is the cleansing and sometimes very painful work of solitude, an absolutely necessary work if we wish to enter into the secret chamber of the heart. Primarily it is God's work, not ours. The God who is at the heart of our being calls us to enter into this solitude so that we might be healed. The grace of contemplation by which we taste sweetly of the divine is the same light by which we enter into the cell of self-knowledge. All of us stand in need, to some degree, of the healing of our human life and the grace to accept our fragility and woundedness.

We fear to face ourselves. We fear our aloneness and vulnerability. Yet only in penetrating our innermost solitude do we reach communion with God. Our loneliness is not alleviated by surrounding ourselves with crowds and noise, because this aloneness is an essential part of our truth. There is no escape from this solitude we carry within us. We conquer it not by denying it or running away from it, but by accepting and embracing it as a means to intimacy. Solitude is an invitation to intimacy. Our longing for intimacy is meant to be fulfilled by the Lord, who dwells in the secret chamber of our heart. The Lord Jesus was sent to tell us that we are loved and that God has called us into the same intimacy that he shares with the Father and the Spirit. Caught up in that love, we too are sent to love as we have been loved.

We can let go of our fears, doubts and anxieties through the healing power of solitude. We need to stop running from fear—the fear of our own finiteness, our inability to control every situation, the limits of our own potentialities. To face our fear is to confront our nothingness, our incompleteness, and to allow confrontation to blossom into encounter. Our response to this encounter is to leap into the abyss of our nothingness, to put all our hope in Another, who has promised to be faithful to us.

We feel safe and secure when we seem to dominate life. This is a false and fragile security. God's fidelity is our only assurance. As we saw earlier, the real process of transformation can begin only when we have entered into the mystery of self-surrender and self-emptying. We must die to the need to be what others ask us to be or what society imposes on us of its false values, so that we may become the beautiful and unique person we have been created to be. God calls us to live to the fullest the truth of who we are. The solitude of the heart, which we carry with us at all times, comes to fruition in an attitude of presence to self, to others and to God. We then manifest this attitude in all we say and do.

God can call us to live this solitude and to experience its healing aspects in the midst of our busiest day. The sense of our incompleteness, loneliness, separateness—or, on the other hand, a sense of peace, love and solidarity with all God's creation—can beckon us to the gift of solitude we hold within. Through our ongoing response, we will gradually be brought into living our life from the heart. We will understand that life, in all its aspects, is to be gathered into the pivotal relationship with God in Christ Jesus.

The prayer of the heart calls us to hide absolutely nothing from God and to surrender unconditionally to his loving mercy.

Conclusion

Surrendering our fears has been a recurring thread in this and previous chapters. We all face so many fears, both interior and exterior. God understands our fears and, in the scriptures, constantly tells us not to be afraid.[39] God walks with us as he walked with Adam and Eve in the intimacy of the garden. When God calls someone into a new place, to begin a new journey, he also assures them of his constant presence with them. God is always faithful.

Our commitment to surrender to God's initiative is always accompanied and supported by grace. We find our home and our belonging in our heart's core because we at last understand how deeply we are loved. This is a love that nothing can take away from us. We also find home and belonging because we are at peace with the truth of ourselves. This is a wonderful gift that, consciously or unconsciously, we all seek.

God, help us to recognise the closed doors in life's journey as portals to the inner chambers of our heart, and give us the courage to open them one by one until we reach that inner heart centre where all is peace and love.

Reflections

Discernment of spirits

How can we distinguish the guidance of the Holy Spirit from other spirits or voices within? The voice of God, even when showing us what needs healing, is always positive and hopeful and does not cause us shame or despair. Negative inner voices that cause us to lose hope are always from the world, the devil and what is wounded and insecure within us.

Pray to the Holy Spirit for the gift of discernment and the humility to receive insights into what is wounded and in need of healing.

9

Freedom to shape our story

We are not just human beings but human becomings… For us to be is to have a lifetime, a development… Our lifetime is a life story. [40]

Our existence is a gift from God to shape according to the truth of our creation. We are shaped by our eternal beginnings: because we come from God, our perfection consists in returning to God. A natural human morality, written on our hearts, is defined by our impetus toward God, as Paul teaches (Romans 2:14–15). In this chapter we will explore the diamond of our humanity from yet another perspective: our moral life and human liberty, the confluence of nature and grace as fulfilling our potential for human excellence.

St Thomas Aquinas taught that the moral life is shaped by where we come from and where we are going. Aquinas shows that the purpose of human life is happiness, and that happiness is a consequence of living according to who we are as created in God's image. We come from God and return to God, who is our destiny. Everything we are and everything we do is sandwiched between these two poles.

We come home to ourselves in going forth from ourselves into God—a familiar theme. A deep-rooted desire to have a place of belonging, a home, is written indelibly on our innermost being and springs from the impetus to return to our source in God.

The fundamental desire of the human heart, recognised or not, is for God. Whether we are saints or sinners, there is a great restlessness in the human spirit for God, by whom and through whom we exist. As Augustine said so eloquently, 'Our hearts are restless till they rest in thee.'[41] Happiness can be found only in fidelity to our faith journey outward to God, who is our beginning.

The moral life, desire and human choice

Our decisions determine how the story of our life will unfold. God leaves us free to move toward or to move sadly away from the destiny written in the core of our being. Human freedom is a concept that has appeared throughout this book, taken up repeatedly in various contexts as an essential component of our humanness. Our freedom is an image of God's freedom and is rooted in that freedom. We are not limited by our obedience to God. Rather, our human potential is brought to completeness in our union with God's purpose for bringing us into existence. How can we be limited by perfection, by a becoming that will fulfil every desire of our hearts? 'It is in surrendering to the alluring call of the divine that we are most free, most ourselves, most at home.'[42]

Our full possession of freedom requires healing and grace because of the wounds and division wrought by sin. God who created us free does not drag us along the way to holiness but always respects the gift of our autonomy. Here we have another of the great paradoxes of our journey to God. By our own efforts we cannot merit grace. At the same time, without our consent, grace cannot enter our hearts.

For our secular world, the most common description of freedom is lack of restrictions—the ability to be self-determining. Some modern moral theologians regard freedom as 'freedom from the constraint of law and authority', which allows the individual to be the determiner of moral good or evil.[43] Human history has proven that if we set ourselves as the determiners of life outside our relationship to God, the consequences are domination, oppression, selfishness and death. Only in communion with God are we able to rule benignly and be one with creation and other human beings. 'When one agrees that the foundations of all moral truth abide in God himself and reflect his wisdom, then... nothing is more real for the human creature than to seek conformity with the truth that exists in God.'[44]

Morality concerns what we have in our heart. 'Heart is a symbol of what we are in ourselves, of the source of all our reactions and aspirations... The heart of our heart is God.'[45] The moral life is fashioned by choices turning us to God. God sustains us in existence in all that we do, even when we choose wrongly. Our sinful choices do not thwart God's plan but only slow us in our growth toward completion. God is ever ready to forgive our sins; his forgiveness does not change God, but us. 'When God forgives our sins, he is not changing his mind about us. He is changing *our* minds about him. He does not change; his mind is never anything but loving; he *is* love.'[46]

To live a life of virtue, developed by habits of choosing to be formed by what is good, what is of God, creates in us a listening heart that is open to all the contemplative graces at work within us through the Holy Spirit.

We become what we desire

For Aquinas, the starting point for the moral life does not involve a list of things we can or cannot do. Instead, he begins with the truth of our creation. In the wonderful theology of Aquinas, the human person is considered in its totality as a body/spirit composite; we are thinking beings who are moved to action through our desires and inner dispositions. 'Our choices, he reasons, are actions which flow from what we, as individuals, are. They reflect our desires and our view of things.'[47] Conversely, our repeated ways of acting shape our dispositions. How we interpret and respond to the world, to the circumstances of our life and to others will depend on what kind of person we are, what virtues or vices we have developed.

Our desires are the gateway to either good or bad actions. It is our motivations and desires that inform and move us toward practical life choices. Virtue 'is a principle of action flowing from our inner dispositions'.[48] Whatever holds sway within us determines our choices, our liberty and who we are. Our actions depend on what has formed our judgment, and our repeated action impacts on how we live our life. We do not live accidental lives. God has created us as free agents with the capacity to make decisions. When we seek what is truly good, then we are seeking God, who is the source of all good.

The diminishment caused by sin

Sin and evil diminish the human person. When we hear about someone torturing another human being, we immediately have an internal sense of something wrong, something out of balance in such a person. We have a standard of rightness for human be-haviour. We have certain expectations of what it means to be good or evil.[49] Moral evil has an effect in the world and on others, but, more fundamentally, the one who sins is diminished. Perhaps we do not reflect enough upon this key point. Our origin in God means that our being and our actions are associated with this divine origin. God's goodness and love are the standard for human action.

If my God is the God of the Bible, the living God, the 'I am, I was, I am coming', then God is inseparable from the world and from human beings… My action, then, consists in handing myself over to my God, who allows me to be the link for his divine activity regarding the world and other people.[50]

Culture is formed by our individual choices, choices that are born not in a vacuum but within the reality of our human becomings:

as we shape ourselves, so we shape our world. It is easy to lose sight of the real power and impact an individual can have on others and on society. Etty Hillesum died in Auschwitz because a culture of death formed by human choices wrought evil for so many. Etty's response to her historical moment took shape through her conscious decision to love and be toward God. Hitler and Etty: their determinations fashioned their individual stories and even beyond. The lives of these two polar opposites affected so many other human stories.

What causes people blindly to follow men and women who are living by evil choices? Could it be a lack of awareness, not being conscious enough of their own integrated worth, and therefore missing the potential and dignity of others? We can return to Aristotle's understanding of self-love as necessary for appreciating the value of the other.

The ability to grasp the truth of a historical moment, the forces and persons who are crafting a particular time, enables us to respond humanly and to choose that which leads to goodness and brings us toward human excellence and perfection.

We have many examples of Christians and non-Christians who have chosen another way in the face of popular opinion and co-ercion: Edith Stein, Maximilian Kolbe, Gandhi and many others who chose to live and die for moral values that are countercultural. What made these individuals different? As Christians, our faith gives us the strength to be courageous in our choices, to follow the example of Jesus, to love as he did. On a more elemental level, for Christian and non-Christian alike, the basic underlying factor comes from a sense of the dignity of the human person: that there is, at the core of every human being, a greatness and goodness that cannot be violated. Our goodness is a created participation in God's goodness.

Made for friendship

A virtuous life is an existence given to relationship, to the gift of ourselves in self-communication to others.

We have a special name for human living with each other. We call it friendship... Friendship is more than people wishing well to other people. It involves what Aquinas calls communication, sharing, *and the New Testament calls* Koinonia, *sharing a common life. Friendship is a matter of being* with *others.*[51]

We can be with others most completely only when we are in communion with God, who is the source of our goodness and our love.

The grace of the Holy Spirit brings us into the communion of friendship within the Trinity. Flowing from our divine friendship with God is our connectedness and loving interaction with one another. Catherine of Siena writes, 'We must dress up in his blazing charity... [and] know within ourselves God's infinite goodness.'[52] Friendship completes us; we are created to be a community of love because we are like God. Our self-communication mirrors the self-communication and self-giving that is the Trinity.

We are like an individual note in a song. The note 'A' has its own definition and reality; without it, music is not possible. Yet each note forms a song by its relation to every other note. Relationship and timing create the harmony, beauty and definition of each musical piece. Living virtuously teaches us to enter into God's harmony by being true to our individual created truth and being inserted into the totality of the song of all creation.

God's action

We can shape our lives through virtuous choices and habits but our effort is never enough without the indwelling Spirit of God. The Holy Spirit has been sent into our heart as the guide for our spiritual journey. The Spirit acts within our spirit, allowing our activity to become one with God's activity. The gifts of the Spirit that are named in Isaiah 11:2—wisdom, understanding, counsel, might, knowledge and the fear of the Lord—perfect our human spirit in following the promptings of God.[53] Through the Spirit, we enter into God's way of knowing and understanding. Aquinas says that 'we are guided by the advice, as it were, of God'.[54] Through the power of the Holy Spirit at work in us, our human capacity for goodness and love is stretched to divine dimensions (John 14:16; 16:13).

I hand myself over to the action of the living God, communicating himself according to his plan, to the world and to other human beings. I can only place myself faithfully before God, and offer the fullness of my being and my resources so that I can be there where God awaits me, the link between this action of God and the world.[55]

The Holy Spirit teaches us to live a graced life in conformity with our unique gift of existence. God works in each of us and in all his creation according to the nature of each.[56] To know God and to love him is the goal of human life. Knowing and loving are mutually inclusive, involving the whole of our person. We have a natural capacity to know and therefore delight in the knowledge of truth. This is the meaning of Aquinas' insight that grace builds upon nature; who we are and the presence of the Holy Spirit in our heart is a bond so intimate that it matters very little if our good thoughts are from our spirit or from God's Spirit dwelling within us. God is so intimate to us that:

It is from within us, deep down within us that the new life proceeds, and that means that anything which is not an expression of us will not be an expression of God either. But in some sense the converse of this is also true. What is not an expression of God will not be an expression of us.[57]

We are a created expression of the truth of God. The healing of grace makes us a transparent reflection of God to others. We are 'clear pools in which God's reality can be mirrored... We are "built for" union with the divine, marked as it were with the stamp of God's being.'[58]

The Spirit helps us in our weakness and teaches us to pray. The Spirit of God intercedes for us and brings us into God's will and plan. The Holy Spirit completes Christ's work in us, which is to transform us into Jesus and bring us into the union shared by Father and Son. The action of the Spirit binds us within this loving union. The life of grace and the indwelling Spirit moves us, teaches us and touches us so that we may know God and give ourselves to him in love. It is through grace, then, that God's activity enters into our human activity.

All Christians are called to live according to the mind and thinking of Jesus Christ: 'Let the same mind be in you that was in Christ Jesus' (Philippians 2:5). In other words, we are to live to the full capacity of our nature, which is to know and to love, and to be perfected by these activities. Our whole being should be motivated by a deep yearning to penetrate the truths of God so that we may surrender more fully to God in contemplative love.

The truths and the knowledge we receive in contemplation are the beginning of the perfect knowledge that is eternal life. John writes in his Gospel, 'And this is eternal life, that they may know you, the only true God, and Jesus Christ whom you have sent' (17:3). The end and fulfilment of human perfection is being possessed by God. Paul explains, 'Now I know only in part; then I will know fully, even as I have been fully known' (1 Corinthians 13:12).

Conclusion

What is the true end to which the human person is destined? There can be only one answer: God. Only in God, whom we image, can we find completion and happiness. What is good is defined by our life in God. Evil and sin bind us in the land of 'unlikeness', which the story of Adam and Eve's alienation from God and from all creation makes clear. The exercise of virtue liberates us to love. We move from a wounded, broken need to be loved to the freedom of a person who loves, who is in communication with others, and who is capable of friendship.

Human virtue is completed by grace, which is a participation in the life of God. The grace of Jesus Christ and the gifts of the Holy Spirit are constantly knocking at the door of our hearts for entrance. Our response to God's grace is receptivity to the Holy Spirit, which directs us toward all that is good and excellent. The Spirit fills our thirsting spirit with the love that surpasses understanding. Ultimately, it is love that moves us to action.

Reflections

On new habits and virtue

Forming new habits changes our behaviour and the way we act. In what areas of your life do you feel that you are held in bondage? Choose one habitual action that you would like to change. Developing virtuous action starts with the decision to change just one thing and the resolve to persevere in doing so. In the end, God's grace will heal and transform us.

Part 3
The last word: re-creation in Christ

I stand alone on the mountain
and look out upon a rocky field.
The Voice calls to me:
'Who will till and plant my field?'
The invitation pierces my heart
like a two-edged sword.
The field is vast and I plant alone.
Is there no other way?
Must someone always go before?
Must someone always die
in the secret places
of the barren earth?
Must someone have for companion
only the hidden, silent stream
of God's life-giving Word?
No other comfort but this
—and must that someone be I?
I opened my hands
to receive the seed
that would bring life
and greenness to God's field
—and death to me.

10
Mary: the place of new creation

In the beginning when God created the heavens and the earth, the earth was a formless void and darkness covered the face of the deep.
GENESIS 1:1–2

In the beginning, God spoke. To repeat a mantra voiced in earlier chapters, God created all things by his Word and breathed into them his Spirit: creation came forth from God's being. God spoke and we were made. God breathed into us a unique likeness to the divine essence. In the garden the serpent echoed God's promise, saying 'You shall be like God', but in a sense that God had not intended. The serpent's words were a lie and our unmaking. God spoke again, at the foreordained time, a final Word—Jesus, who would bring a new creation to birth. God's Word now has a human face.

Hush, a silent world awaits
a word of healing—a word of hope.
The Word leapt down and found
a waiting emptiness, a void,
open to a new creative
uttering of God's Word:
the receptive heart
of a young girl.

The coming of the Word

The advent of the Word in the womb of the virgin Mary was the privileged moment of our new creation. Mary is the first fruit of the redemption. Mary is the new Eve who, through her obedience, opened herself to the fruitfulness of the Holy Spirit. The fruit of her womb brings re-creation to all God's people. The birth of the Word of God from her womb has overcome death and given us rebirth into new life in God through the indwelling Spirit.

Mary's 'yes' at the annunciation freed all humanity from bondage to sin and death. Mary is the perfect human response to God and the pattern for becoming a new creation in Christ. She is the mother of God and also the first disciple of her son. Mary's vocation is unique, of course, yet at the same time it is the vocation of every Christian disciple to bear the Word of God in the inner chamber of their heart and to give birth to that Word for the salvation of others.

In the annunciation scene, then, we have a portrait of God's initiative and human response. The story of our re-creation reveals God's intimate work in the human person as trinitarian: the Father who speaks a promise, the overshadowing of the Holy Spirit, and the birth of the Word of God in time. Catherine of Siena writes of this moment:

In you today is written the eternal Father's wisdom; in you today our human strength and freedom are revealed. I say that our human dignity is revealed because if I look at you, Mary, I see that the Holy Spirit's hand has written the Trinity in you by forming within you the incarnate Word, God's only-begotten Son.[59]

In Mary we at last understand the full dignity of the human person created in God's image. The Word of God conceived in Mary's womb through the power of the Holy Spirit is the same Word conceived in our hearts through the Holy Spirit. In her Magnificat, Mary proclaims the joy of being filled with the Spirit, the joy of her spirit abundantly reflecting God's Spirit. She manifests true humility, acknowledging both God's greatness in her and her own human lowliness. Mary is an untarnished mirror of God's holiness. She is God's lowly servant. To be a servant of the Most High is to be a disciple, a follower of Jesus, who said that he had come 'not to be served but to serve' (Mark 10:45).

Mary believed that the Holy Spirit could bring about God's promise, as outlandish as it might have seemed. Her 'yes' gave the Spirit access to do the work of God in her; that work of grace was directed toward the salvation of all created reality.

Open receptivity

Before Jesus was conceived in her womb, Mary's heart was a hollowed receptivity, waiting for God's formative word. Caryll Houselander describes Mary's pre-advent waiting as emptiness: 'Not a formless emptiness like a void without meaning; on the contrary it has a shape, a form given to it by the purpose for which it is intended.'[60] Mary's emptiness has a shape. It is not the formless void of the first creation but a form fitted to her particular call to discipleship: to be the place of God's re-creation.

Here again we are faced with the mystery of emptiness—a new understanding of emptiness—as we ponder what it means in God's mother. Understanding Mary's emptiness enables us to see more clearly to what we are being called. We need to enter into the process of being divested of our sinfulness by rebirth in baptism and the inflowing grace of the Holy Spirit, which progressively effects in us that original empty receptivity before God. We all need emptying of something; we are all wounded and need to return to the first state of innocence that opens our heart to receive God. Or perhaps it is better to say that we need to recognise the God who is with us always.

As in Mary's case, our inner space and the process of emptying will reflect the purpose of our mission in the world. Mary's emptiness is 'like the hollow in the reed, the narrow riftless emptiness which can have only one destiny: to receive the piper's breath and to utter the song that is in his heart... She was a reed through which the Eternal Love was to be piped as a shepherd's song.'[61] A reed through which God's eternal love is breathed forth in the Son.

The emptiness of Mary is not the vacant meaninglessness of our secular culture, which, rather than being a receptacle for the divine, is so often a void filled only with small desires and sensual pleasures that try to substitute for the rich emptiness that waits for God.

Because of sin, our desires need to be brought into conformity with God's desire for us. Our actions flow from our desires: 'One is tempted by one's own desire, being lured and enticed by it; then, when that desire has conceived, it gives birth to sin, and that sin, when it is fully grown, gives birth to death' (James 1:14–15).

God cannot be blamed for what is wrong in our world; these problems stem from our divided hearts and inordinate desires. Through grace, we have the capacity to allow the work of the Holy Spirit to purify our desires and direct them to God and salvation. When Mary gave birth to life, the world was set free from death and brought into a godly participation in giving the God-life to the world.

Mary, model of discipleship

Mary is the perfect disciple. She teaches us how to make of our hearts an empty void into which the Word may be spoken for our salvation and for the salvation of all God's people. All who are in God are called to a mission, personal and yet universal, by which we become conduits in the world for God's salvific grace. Mary's divine motherhood is her personal graced vocation as a disciple. In the rhythm of God's grace and Mary's response, we have a map for the spiritual journey.

There are many interconnecting themes between the sending

of the Spirit on Mary at the annunciation and the sending of the Spirit on the believers at Pentecost. Before Jesus ascends to the Father, he promises the gift of the Holy Spirit to his disciples. We are those disciples. Through the power of the Holy Spirit we are called to be witnesses of God's love in the world.

When the day of Pentecost had come, they were all together in one place. And suddenly from heaven there came a sound like the rush of violent wind, and it filled the entire house where they were sitting. Divided tongues, as of fire, appeared among them, and a tongue rested on each of them. (Acts 2:1–3)

At Pentecost, the Holy Spirit overshadows the apostles individually in the form of tongues of fire. Just as the Spirit overshadowed Mary at the annunciation to bring her into the fullness of the vocation prepared for her from God, the apostles are overshadowed by God's Spirit, effecting in them the fullness of their vocation to preach and witness to the truth of the Word of God, Jesus.

The gifts of the Holy Spirit are given to individuals for the sake of the community. The Spirit descends upon the gathered believers with power, coming like the rush of a violent wind. The Spirit's coming is described as divided tongues of fire resting on each of the believers—divided and distributed. Each individual is gifted by the Spirit, but there is only one fire, from which each receives a part.

Conclusion

We are chosen and called to love and to bear fruit through the Spirit of God. Discipleship and fruitfulness are inseparable. An important part of this fruitfulness is becoming witnesses of the truth (John 15:27). 'You did not choose me but I chose you. And I appointed you to go and bear fruit, fruit that will last' (v. 16).

Mary's mission to be Word-bearer affects all of God's children.

She received power from on high to achieve God's purpose in her life. Each of us receives a divine call that can not only change us as individuals but can change our world, our time, our workspace and our small part of creation. This is our profound Christian hope as disciples.

Reflections

On discipleship and mission

Reflect on the truth that, like Mary, each of us has been called to a unique mission of discipleship. Perhaps your call is to be involved with church ministry, to serve the poor, or to be a contemplative presence in the world.

Pray to the Holy Spirit, asking to understand your particular work in God's plan. Make a list of your particular gifts for service. These gifts will flow from the unique person you are. Reflect on each gift, offering yourself to God's service.

11
The God who dwells within

The first thing to say about… Christian prayer, the prayer of the Church, is that it is just the life of God, the life of the Trinity lived out in us.[62]

We began this book with a reflection on nature, the human person and the meaning of human happiness. This reflection offered a foundation for understanding that the true place of prayer is the human person created in God's image. The place of God's personal dwelling is in our innermost being. In this final chapter we want to reflect on who this God is who dwells in our inner room. We may see God as a rather generic entity, all-powerful and separate from us, yet our God is a personal God. Jesus reveals the God who brought us into existence, continues to sustain us and, more astonishingly, has entered into a personal relationship of love with us, his creatures.

The fourth Gospel, the Gospel according to John, will be the source we draw on as we complete our teaching on prayer as a relationship both with God and with our sisters and brothers. The two relationships are inseparable, just as contemplation is inseparable from activity. The icon of St Dominic's life clearly illustrates this truth.

The prologue of the fourth Gospel, which describes our re-creation in Christ, echoes the creation story in Genesis. It was through his Word that God created the heavens and the earth and humankind. Jesus is God's Word who now speaks with a human voice and brings about a renewed creation by entering into that very creation (1:14, 18). John wants to root the birth of Jesus in the Genesis story of creation and retell it in the context of our re-creation in Christ. 'In the beginning was the Word, and the Word was with God, and the Word was God. He was in the beginning with God. All things came into being through him, and without him not one thing came into being' (John 1:1–3).

The Gospel account of our new creation unveils more fully the nature of God and God's presence within us and the divine action in our life.

Trinitarian indwelling

Prayer is the life of the Trinity lived in us. It is the mystery of God making his home in us. Trying to say something about the Trinity is a rather daunting task. For many, the Trinity is a doctrine formulated by the church, a mystery beyond our understanding. To some extent there is truth in that doctrine, but the full truth is so much more. Our God is a personal God who reaches down to us and has been revealed to us by Jesus as Trinity. Knowing God cannot be a closed door. It is God's Holy Spirit who continues to reveal to us, through an inner encounter, who God is. We study and try to learn more about our faith, but that is not the end of it: God comes to us in love, and in that encounter we touch God. As prayer deepens, we know God in love beyond words—a true knowing of the heart, a contemplative experience open to everyone. Jesus, in John's Gospel, does not say 'I will come to a chosen few'; rather, his promise is to anyone who loves him: God—Father, Son and Holy Spirit—will come and dwell with them.

Jesus frequently speaks of receiving, obeying and abiding in his word, in relation to the Father and to the gift of the Holy Spirit.

Our spiritual journey depends on hearing, receiving and acting upon God's word and receiving the gift of the Holy Spirit as our guide, comforter and advocate.

Jesus is the Word of God who speaks to us the words of salvation and desires that we remain in his word. He does not speak on his own behalf but relates only what he has heard and received from the Father. John shows the effects of Jesus' words and teaching in the believer: 'Very truly, I tell you, anyone who hears my word and believes him who sent me has eternal life, and does not come under judgment, but has passed from death to life' (5:24).

We can come to the Father only through the healing and transforming power of Jesus' word. Conversely, if we do not receive his word, we have no part in the Father or the Spirit (8:47). When we receive the word, we in turn share that word with others and become one with the life-giving action of the Word. Like Mary, we become the reed or conduit that brings forth the Word. We are sent to speak God's word to others through the power of the Spirit (3:34).

It is the Spirit who brings to fruition the gift of salvation within us and through us, as disciples in the world. The Spirit is the gift given to us by the Father and the Son, whereby a full working out of the communion between Father and Son is accomplished in us as a permanent gift. The Spirit guides and teaches us how to be disciples of Jesus, intercedes in us for the salvation of all, and equips us to do the work of God in the world. 'When the Spirit of truth comes, he will guide you into all the truth; for he will not speak on his own, but will speak whatever he hears, and he will declare to you the things that are to come' (16:13).

The Spirit continues to share Jesus' teaching with us. Just as Jesus spoke only what he heard from the Father, so too the Spirit teaches only what comes from Jesus. We have here, then, a pattern for the salvific work of the whole Trinity in time and in our hearts. The Father loves us because we have believed that Jesus came from God.

We follow the same pattern. We, too, have come from the Father; and at the completion of our earthly existence we, too, will return to the Father. Jesus, in his coming from God and in his return to God, has conquered the world. Nothing is the same any more. This is our faith. How does this truth become a life-forming conviction within us? Through the coming of Jesus we become heirs with him by faith, partakers in the divine nature. In baptism we are taken into the divine unity of communion: as the Father and Son are one, so we are one in them.

Created for communion

We are created in the image of God who is Trinity, a communion of three distinct persons in the unity of one divine nature. We are somehow like God, whose existence is an eternal relationship of reciprocal self-giving and communication. 'Each person of the Trinity exists for and from each other. Their names do not separate them off from each other but show that the Triune God is pure relationship... For God "to be" is "to-be-related".'[63] God fashioned us in the beginning with the capacity for communion; by the grace given to us in Christ Jesus, God enables us to enter into the divine communion of love.

Our creation in God's image both constitutes the source of personal fulfilment and bestows the task of seeking unity and solidarity with others. We are created as unique and individual, as well as social, beings. Both of these realities find their source in the triune God. Our love of other human beings is irrevocably rooted in our union with and likeness to God. 'Those who say, "I love God", and hate their brothers or sisters, are liars; for those who do not love a brother or sister whom they have seen, cannot love God whom they have not seen' (1 John 4:20).

Our whole existence as persons can be defined in terms of interrelatedness: with God in whom we find completion, with other men and women, and with the universe. By our very nature we are called to intimacy with God and with others. God's gift to us is a fundamental capacity for communion.

We are made in God's image not only because each individual is like God as a thinking and free being, but also because, in our common humanity, we are called to live in a communion of love. This communion reflects in the created world the communion of love that is in God. Such love is the whole content of Jesus' message in the Gospel (see John 17:22–23) and the source of the church's teaching on justice among peoples and nations. Social justice is not a modern phenomenon; it is rooted in the very nature of God and imprinted on our nature as those who are completed only through our relationship to one another. Human solidarity finds its source in the trinitarian communion.

'Communication' is such a common word in our vocabulary. Sadly, so much of this communication is via the internet and can lack true interpersonal communication. The kingdom is already here in seed through the loving action of those who live the God-life in practical deeds of self-giving love and service to their neighbour. Each one of us is so important for the reign of God here and now. Because I am a cloistered nun, I do not travel often. A few years ago, I had to go to a meeting of Dominican nuns in Washington, DC. On the return trip to my monastery, I was stranded all day in several airports because of bad weather. My affiliation is quite visible, as I wear a religious habit. From 6 a.m. to 7 p.m., a constant stream of people came up to talk to me. The people I spoke to were of a variety of ages and interests—Catholics, New Agers and the merely curious; at one point, a mother even woke me up to talk with her little boy. These encounters were not about me but about God, whom they saw me representing.

My Dominican habit made it very easy for me to give love and attention to each of these individuals. In our often impersonal and busy culture, I believe that a smile or an act of kindness makes us stand out and witness to a spiritual dimension even without a habit—like the woman who offered me the use of her mobile phone to let my sisters know I would be late. Not often, but some-times, being in a religious habit has brought me a frown or look of disapproval, which is, for me, a challenge to send out love all the more. Our love and kindness are not dependent on others' acceptance, but only on the God who seeks to love and be in communication with others through us.

The unity of Jesus and his Father in the love of the Holy Spirit is given to us as the form of Christian perfection and the apex of our life of prayer. The trinitarian unity is both model and source of the unity of believers, and so it can be said that our unity has its origin in the divine life and action. Our individual perfection is completed through the building up of the communion of persons that constitutes the body of Christ called together in the one Spirit. Our unity in Jesus is meant to be a living icon of the Trinity.

When we speak of our likeness to God, we must always speak in terms of something that, in some mysterious way, is like and at the same time radically different from God. Our self-giving and self-communication to one another are necessarily incomplete and imperfect, a dim though real reflection of the unity that is God's nature. We, though many, become one as we enter into the mystery of God by loving and giving ourselves in love. The truth of the human person includes relationship—a concept that goes against the modern understanding of the human person defined by a philosophy of individualism.

In the abiding presence of God-with-us, we are called into divine friendship, which is the source of our friendship with one another. In this way, by following the law of Christ, which is love, we reveal God, who is love. Seeking peace, justice and the good of others is a fundamental part of our existence as individuals. In such a community of friendship, rooted in the Spirit, the dignity of each person is recognised.

In imitation of Jesus, we are called to love the other even in the face of a loveless return. In John's Gospel, Jesus gives a new com-mandment: to love one another as he has loved us (John 13:34).

When just one person realises this tremendous mission to love, it makes the world a better place. God continues to make this mission of love real in countless women and men—yesterday, today and throughout the centuries until Jesus' return.

Thus, through the New Testament revelation, we see from the interpersonal love in the Trinity what human love in God's image is meant to be. It is the indwelling Spirit who makes us one. The continuing work of unity is effected through the Spirit, who is the source of unity and also the source of diversity and giftedness. It is the Spirit who brings to completion in believers the unity that is like the union between the Father and the Son.

Conclusion

In the image of the vine and the branches, we see how close our connection to God is. We received life from God and we continue to exist only in relation to the inflowing sap of the God-life. Our actions in the world bear fruit in relation to the abiding presence of the Trinity within us. It is Jesus' word, which we have heard and assimilated, that cleanses us (John 15:3).

His promise to each of us is that if his word truly abides in us, we can ask for what we need. Our prayer is answered because our asking is in God. We intercede for the world from within the plan of God; we groan with the eternal longing of God for the salvation of all creation, which has already been accomplished in the death and resurrection of Jesus. The word abiding in us is not a passive experience but one that moves us to do the action of God in the world.

In the beginning, God created everything in goodness; we sinned and God re-created. Thus we have been brought full circle. We come forth from our source and return to that source: God who is our beginning and end.

Reflections

Being and doing

Reflect on the interconnectedness of contemplation and action, on human solidarity having its source in God: that our practical deeds of self-giving love manifest the reign of God already present here and now.

Put this truth into practice through specific concrete action: for example, helping a neighbour with a project, or giving time, not just money, to a charitable cause. Self-giving love is an act of donating our very self to others in service.

Study and reflect on John's Gospel, particularly those passages where the Trinity is implied (chapters 14—17). Read through these chapters several times. Then choose a few verses to meditate on, praying to the Holy Spirit for guidance to understand Jesus' words and for the gift of encounter with the God within.

Conclusion: Of prayer and life

In writing this book, I wanted to show that prayer is not about how well we learn certain methods or exercises. Prayer is about bringing God—the God in whom we exist and move and have our being—into our daily routine. Authentic prayer reveals a deep integrity between who we are in God's presence and who we are with one another, who we are when we worship in church and what we do after worship. Prayer is meant to shape our whole life. To pray is to live life in a new way.

Life is a road—a highway, as Isaiah teaches (35:8). God's highway is the one road that leads us back to God, to glory. Jesus is the highway and the Holy Spirit the guide and keeper of the correct signposts along the way. The destination is the Father and participation in the cycle of trinitarian life. To choose Christ is to choose to be a disciple each day and to walk the section of the highway we are called to travel that day. The road is not always straight: there are crossroads and detours. But if we open our heart to the promptings of the Holy Spirit, we will traverse the way safely.

Every person is called to prayer because we belong to God and are created in God's image. It is not enough to be 'pray-ers'; we are to be the place of God's presence for the world, the receptacle containing God's salvation for all peoples. We meet all humanity within the inner room of our heart. Etty Hillesum touches upon the limitless scope of being a God-bearer when she says, 'There are no frontiers between suffering people, and we must pray for them all.'[64] Each day is a new opportunity to enter into the heart of God and his divine plan of love.

Throughout human history, God has chosen individuals such as Abraham, Peter, Paul, Antony of the desert, Claire, Dominic and Etty Hillesum to live the journey with particular intensity and understanding so that others may follow with courage and hope. We are chosen to make the journey, to enter into the mystery of letting go and going forth from our comfortable ways of being into the God-adventure. The journey is always surprising, stretching us to our full human potential as lovers of life, beauty and truth. The place of our encounter is where we live our life and the people we rub shoulders with, day in and day out. We cannot be missionaries to the world until we have learned to be happy and to find God in the place where we are at this moment.

Unceasing prayer is a daily relationship with God, one that leads us in love to an encounter with our neighbour. In God and with others and all creation, we will one day enter into the fullness of communion, into the eternal symphony of joyous praise. This is not the end but truly only the beginning.

Appendix
Formed by God's word

Much of this book has been dedicated to exploring the ways we are transformed by God's word. The various witnesses and traditions of prayer cited and reflected upon demonstrate how a faith response to the word of God brings us to holiness.

The privileged place of encounter is to hear the word proclaimed in the liturgy and respond to that proclamation in faith, opening our hearts to the life-giving presence of Jesus. God speaking to us is at the focal point of our spiritual journey and our life of prayer. God, in Christ and through the power of the Holy Spirit, speaks to us in the liturgy. The gift of our baptism incorporates us into full liturgical participation as God's priestly people.

The church's liturgy is meant to be a special place of transformation. Attending church is not simply about sitting in a pew, watching the priest or listening passively to the scriptures. Liturgy is an active experience where God calls the community and each individual to participate consciously in what happens. The liturgy works in the depths of our minds and hearts a very gradual, barely perceptible transformation of who we are, so quietly that we might easily think that nothing is happening at all.[65] Our liturgical celebrations continue to be active, even urgent, conversion experiences that invite us into discipleship. We need to relearn how to be present to God, who waits for us.

Prayer and ritual

Being comfortable with using our bodies for prayer is important. The rituals of the liturgy are directed to the involvement of the whole person, body and spirit, in prayer.

Human beings need ritual. From the beginning of our existence, we have created ritual and set aside sacred spaces in which to worship: sacred forests, mountains, temples and churches. Worship in spirit is complete only when our worship finds expression through the words and gestures of our body. The reverent and intentional gestures of worship can become profound prayer without words that unites us to God. This prayer occurs when our gestures are intentional, such as inclining our heads at the name of Jesus, standing for the Gospel, making the sign of the cross on our forehead, lips and heart before the Gospel is proclaimed, and crossing ourselves at other times during the liturgy. Consciously entering into these gestures as a way of worship brings us into the divine presence. Our body can lead our spirit to prayer. The gestures of the Mass are not meaningless: they are designed to allow our spirit to express itself through our bodily presence.

Studying the scriptures

In order to enter fully into God's word during the liturgy, we must prepare. Becoming familiar with the sacred text is an excellent way to ready ourselves to hear the word of God in an active sense. Through study, prayerful reading and reflection, the words of scripture enter into our minds and shape our thinking. We need to saturate ourselves in the language and spirit of the scriptures.

The sacred books teach us who God is, who we are, and what our relationship to God means. In the scriptures we learn the lesson of God's faithful and steadfast love in the face of human weakness and sin. God's revealed word is given to us so that we may understand how to respond to God in such a way as to live in God now and for all eternity.

There are many ways to make scripture a key part of our lives. Learning about the genres, historical background and formation of the books of the Bible is important. But reading about scripture cannot replace grappling with the text itself. We want to find a home in the sacred word.

Take time to read the scriptures every day, alone and as a family, if possible. Study the word of God as it unfolds in the sacred books. Study the sacred word contained in the Old Testament so that you can understand the message of God's saving grace and loving intervention in the lives of men and women of those times, and so that you apply it to our lives today. Such a study is fruitful when the word proceeds from our understanding into our hearts and then into the choices we make and the actions that define our lives as God-centred. All the stories of individuals in both the Old and New Testaments are stories of God's call, human response, conversion and finally transformation, affecting not only the individual but the church and the whole world.

A study method for interacting with the texts

We begin with a careful reading of the text to understand the author's intent. A good study Bible that offers introductions to each book and footnotes to the text can help us understand the historical background of the text and the author's purpose in writing. as we immerse ourselves in reading the scriptures rather than relying on scripture commentaries.

Our first objective in studying a text must be to discover the sense that the original author intended. Reflect on the following questions.

- What is the meaning of this event according to the author?
- What teaching is the author trying to impart to readers of the time?

- What happened in this event, in this particular story?
- Who are the main characters and what is the interaction among them?
- How is God featured in the author's story?
- What message do we receive from the teaching of the author?

The inspired author is often addressing three historical moments:

- The time in which a particular event occurred.
- The time in which the author wrote about the events. It is important to keep in mind that the books of the Bible had a long period of oral tradition before they were written down and gathered into the Bible we now use. For example, the first five books of the Old Testament (the Pentateuch), which serve as an introduction, were written down many centuries after the exodus event and the exile to Babylon. These five books are a reflection on the relationship of God to Israel, which is meant to give those in exile (and, by extension, us) hope in God's unbroken fidelity.
- The time we are living in: this relates to the message the sacred text has for us.

All of these three historical moments are interconnected and formative for God's people here and now.

It is important also to see the relationships between the various books of the Bible. We can see these connections by comparing various books and doing thematic and word studies.

The second important aspect of this study method is to ask questions of the text. These questions help us focus on and interact with the text. Some suggested questions are listed below. As you use this method, more questions will occur to you.

- What is the story teaching? The stories of the Old Testament are not simply relaying historical facts but are recounting the mystery of God's presence in human history, the life of God and the history of the world.

- Ask yourself: What does this section reveal about God? What does it reveal about human beings?
- What is God's response in the face of human sinfulness?
- What do words such as 'steadfast love', 'righteousness', 'justice' and 'mercy' mean? Take note of repeated or significant words in a text. Taking a particular word, such as 'righteousness', and tracing it from the Old Testament into the New Testament can be an enriching and surprising process. This approach allows the scripture to comment on itself.
- What does God's interaction with the various characters of the story teach about the relationship between God and his chosen ones—about the spiritual journey?
- What impact does a deeper understanding of God's word in the scriptures have on my faith journey?

Put this method to work to engage with the text. For example, make a study of the book of Genesis:

- Divide the book into sections.
- Read and study the story of Abraham and each of the patriarchs separately.
- After separating and studying the individual stories, go back and read them in the context of the whole chapter, and then in the context of the message of this particular book of scripture. Keep a journal or study notes and jot down your insights.
- What are some of the key words in the text? Which words carry through from story to story?
- Trace some of the themes you find in Genesis into the teaching of the New Testament. (A topical index is helpful for the study.[66])

Exploring sections thematically

There are many ways to divide a book of the Bible into sections. The following example can help you divide the texts into study sections. This study can be done alone or in a small group.

The creation story (Genesis 1:1—2:3)

Take time to focus on the story of creation: study and pray over the text. Notice the two versions of the creation of human beings; compare them. What does the author teach us about the nature of God? What do you learn of our nature, of our relationship to God and to others, and to all creation?

Primeval history (Genesis 2:4—11:26)

What do we learn of God's faithfulness and human sin? This section gives us an overview of God's desire for us, our sin, and the consequences of being outside God's will. The biblical story gives understanding of the history of the Old Testament, the need for redemption, and God's faithfulness—all of which continues to help us understand what it means to be God-centred in our present culture and society.

This section can be divided further, starting with the theme of sinfulness (Genesis 2—6):

- Adam and Eve in Eden (ch. 2)
- The fall and its consequences (ch. 3)
- The progression of sin (4:1–16)
- Genealogies of Cain (4:17–26) and Seth (ch. 5)
- God's response to human sinfulness (6:1–8)

Continue with the theme of the flood and the spread of nations (Genesis 6—11):

- Noah's preparation for the flood—following God's directives (6:9—7:10)

- God's judgment on human sinfulness and the redemption of the faithful remnant (7:11—8:19)
- The flood's consequences (8:20—9:29)
- The spread of the nations (10:1—11:26)

Patriarchal history (Genesis 11:27—50:26)
These beautiful stories of our biblical ancestors teach about God's choice of individuals for the sake of his people. We see both God's continued faithfulness to the covenant, and the fragility and weakness of those who carry his promises, culminating in the story of Joseph, who foreshadows Christ as one sent to save his family.

Read each section carefully. Notice the way God is defined by the author, and God's interaction with the various characters in the stories.

- How do Abraham, Jacob and Joseph grow into God's call?
- How do the events of their respective journeys mould and form them to God's purpose?
- How do they become leaders for others?

Subdivide this section further, beginning with the life of Abraham (11:27—25:18):

- Abraham's background (11:27–32)
- Abraham's call and response (ch. 12—14)
- Abraham's faith and God's covenant (ch. 15—22)
- Abraham's death (23:1—25:11)
- The descendants of Ishmael (25:12–18)

Continue with the life of Jacob (25:19—35:29):

- Jacob and Esau: Jacob the usurper (25:19—27:46)
- Jacob's search for a wife, and his servitude (ch. 28—30)
- Jacob's return (ch. 31—35)
- The descendants of Esau (36:1—37:1)

Finish with the life of Joseph (37:2—50:26):

- Joseph in Egypt (37:2—41:57)
- Jacob's migration to Egypt (ch. 42—47)
- Jacob's final days and death (48:1—50:14)
- Joseph's final days and death (50:15–26)

This method can be used for the books of both Old and New Testaments. Studying the scriptures in this way helps us to make the sacred word our own: it becomes a living Word, forming and transforming us.

Sacred reading

The sacred text is not a dead letter but a living encounter with God. Studying the scripture is good preparation not only for participation in the liturgy but also for the practice of sacred reading. This ancient monastic practice involves prayerful reading of scripture that becomes a dialogue with God.

The method for sacred reading is simple. Create a quiet space in your day and decide on how long you will engage with the text. Fixing a length of time provides the discipline of waiting for God to speak (15 or 20 minutes is fine). What if God does not seem to speak? Be patient. God is there and will communicate with us. We need to make the space, trust and grow accustomed to the manner in which God manifests himself to us.

It also helps to make a special place where you can do your reading. Set aside a room or a small part of a room as a prayer corner. Display an icon or sacred image there to set the tone. Before beginning the reading, make a bodily gesture, such as bowing or kissing the scripture as a sign that you are approaching God. Take one line or phrase from the scripture and sit quietly, holding this word in your heart. In the silence, let the word itself speak its meaning. Carry over this one word or thought into the day. Just a quick mental recalling of the word or insight received can bring us back to our God-centredness, even in the midst of the busiest day. This practice of the early monastic tradition is accessible to us all.

We live in a culture of instant and often superficial communication. We are no longer a culture of the written word or of knowledge that is savoured and pondered. We are bombarded with a vast assortment of information on any subject by the media and computer technology. Often, this information remains on the surface of our thinking rather than calling us into self-understanding or a contemplative stance. Our grasp of truth and reality can be superficial, and may even prevent us from realising our full potential as reflective beings.

Sacred reading is different from a quick search for information. It is about profoundly interacting with the text as an experience of the living God. We enter into a dialogue with God. God speaks his word in our heart so that a radical transformation can take place. Frequent reading and continual meditation on scripture are an indispensable part of prayer, filling our memory with God. The purpose is to transform our hearts by bringing God to mind throughout the day.

Conclusion

We are created to be *toward God*; our human completeness rests in eternally sharing in God's life.

Both the study of the scriptures and sacred reading help us to discover the gift of salvation offered in the word of God, and the gift of self-knowledge contained in being familiar with the message of the scriptures. It is through interaction with the word—taking it in, memorising it and allowing it to interact with our thoughts, memories and desires—that we reach true self-understanding and are transformed into the likeness of that word.

'The word of God is living and active, sharper than any two-edged sword, piercing until it divides soul from spirit, joints from marrow; it is able to judge the thoughts and intentions of the heart'

(Hebrews 4:12). The word of God is powerful. It enters our hearts and pierces our very depths, cleaving away all that is not God. What remains is a new possession of all that is most dear and the gift of freedom to be who we are.

When we know the scriptures, they then have the power to form and change us.

Reflections

On hearing and praying the scriptures

The liturgy of the church offers a powerful experience of hearing and receiving God's word. Think about learning to pray or participate in the Liturgy of Hours, individually or in a group/parish setting. Do sacred reading of scripture on your own, and begin a serious study of it. Consider beginning or joining a Bible study group.

Read the Post-Synodal Apostolic Exhortation Verbum Domini of Benedict XVI (To the Bishops, Clergy, Consecrated Persons, and the Lay Faithful on the Word of God in the Life and Mission of the Church).[67] Make a note of any new insights you find there.

Notes

1. Simon Tugwell, OP, *The Beatitudes: Soundings in Christian Traditions* (Templegate, 1980), p. 97.
2. Aristotle, *The Nicomachean Ethics*, Introduction by David Ross (Oxford University Press, 1980), p. 29.
3. Mortimer J. Adler, *Aristotle for Everybody: Difficult Thought Made Easy* (Collier, 1978), pp. 69–75.
4. A.H. Armstrong, *An Introduction to Ancient Philosophy* (Rowan & Allanheld, 1983), pp. 107–109.
5. Tugwell, *Beatitudes*, p. 97.
6. Catherine of Siena, *The Dialogue*, translated and introduction by Suzanne Noffke, OP (Paulist Press, 1980), p. 365. Further references to this work will appear in the text.
7. Raymond of Capua, *The Life of St Catherine of Siena* (Tan Books, 1980), pp. 79–88.
8. Augustine, quoted in *Purity of Heart in Early Ascetic and Monastic Literature: Essays in Honor of Juana Raach, OSB* (Liturgical Press, 1999), p. 190.
9. *The Sayings of the Desert Fathers: The Alphabetical Collection*, translated by Benedicta Ward, SLG (Cistercian Publications, 1975), p. xxiv.
10. *The Lives of the Desert Fathers*, translated by Norman Russell (Cistercian Publications, 1981), p. 29.
11. William Harmless, SJ, *Desert Christians: An Introduction to the Literature of Early Monasticism* (Oxford University Press, 2004), pp. 115–141.
12. Douglas Burton-Christie, 'The Geography of the Heart', in *Purity of Heart*, p. 46.
13. Douglas Burton-Christie, *The Word in the Desert: Scripture and the Quest for Holiness in Early Christian Monasticism* (Oxford University Press, 1993), pp. 231–233.
14. *The Lives of the Desert Fathers*, Vol. IX, 'On Amoun', pp. 80–81.
15. 'The Life of Onnophrius', in *Journeying into God: Seven Early Monastic Lives*, translated by Tim Vivian (Fortress, 1996), p. 178.
16. *Athanasius: The Life of Antony and the Letter to Marcellinus* (Paulist Press, 1980), p. 42. St Antony was born around the year 251 and lived in the desert of Egypt.
17. Simon Tugwell, OP, *Ways of Imperfection: An Exploration of Christian Spirituality* (Templegate, 1985), p. 15.

18. Benedicta Ward, SLG, *Harlots of the Desert: A Study of Repentance in Early Monastic Sources* (Cisterican Studies, 1987), p. 104.

19. Tugwell, *Beatitudes*, p. 97.

20. John Cassian, *The Conferences*, translated by Boniface Ramsey (Paulist Press, 1997) conf. 9,2.

21. Vivian, *Journey into God*, pp. 3–4.

22. Michael Ende, *The Never-ending Story* (Dutton Children's Books, 1997), p. 359.

23. Columba Stewart, OSB, 'The Desert Fathers on Radical Self-Honesty', in *Vox Benedicta* (1991), pp. 7–54.

24. See Guy Bedouelle, OP, *Saint Dominic: The Grace of the Word* (Ignatius Press, 1982), pp. 89–103, 215–220.

25. *Saint Dominic: Biographical Documents*, edited by Francis C. Lehner, OP (Thomist Press, 1964), Libellus, pp. 6, 7.

26. Lehner, *Saint Dominic*, p. 7.

27. Lehner, *Saint Dominic*, p. 13.

28. Paul Murray, OP, *The New Wine of Dominican Spirituality: A Drink Called Happiness* (Burns & Oates, 2006), p. 50.

29. Murray, *New Wine of Dominican Spirituality*, p. 7.

30. Bedouelle, *Saint Dominic*, p. 95.

31. *The Early Dominicans: Selected Writings*, edited by Simon Tugwell, OP (Paulist Press, 1982), pp. 4–6.

32. Murray, *New Wine of Dominican Spirituality*, p. 23.

33. Tugwell, *The Early Dominicans*, Jordan of Saxony, Libellus, p. 109.

34. *Etty: The Letters and Diaries of Etty Hillesum 1941–1943* (Novalis, 2002), p. 488. (Further citations will be referenced as *Etty* and given in the text.) Some parts of this chapter were published previously in *Dominican Monastic Search*, a publication of the Association of Nuns in the United States.

35. All references to Catherine's letters are from *The Letters of Catherine of Siena*, translated and with introduction and notes by Suzanne Noffke, OP (Arizona Center for Medieval and Renaissance Studies), Vol. I & Vol. II (2000), Vol. III (2007), Vol. IV (2008); Letter 1241, to Giovanna di Corrado Maconi, July or August 1376, Vol. II, p. 209.

36. Noffke, *Letters of Catherine of Siena*, Vol. II, p. 208.

37. Noffke, *Letters of Catherine of Siena*, Letter T351, to Pope Urban VI, 30 May 1379, Vol. IV, p. 205.

38. Noffke, *Letters of Catherine of Siena*, Letter T213, to Daniella da Orvieto, mid-October 1378, Vol. III, p. 302.

39. Here are a few examples from the Old Testament: God's journey with Abraham: 'Do not be afraid Abram, I am your shield' (Genesis 15:1); God's journey with Isaac: 'Fear not, I am with you' (26:24); the beautiful, comforting words found in Isaiah, 'Say to those who are of a fearful heart, "Be strong, do not fear!"' (Isaiah 35:4), and 'Do not fear, for I have redeemed you; I have called you by name, you are mine' (43:1). In the New Testament, the message to Mary is 'Do not be afraid, Mary' (Luke 1:30).

40. Herbert McCabe, OP, *God Still Matters* (Continuum, 2002), p. 189.

41. Augustine, *Confessions*, Book 1.1.

42. Robert Barron, *Thomas Aquinas: Spiritual Master* (Crossroad, 1996), p. 161.

43. Michael S. Sherwin, OP, *By Knowledge and By Love* (Catholic University of America Press, 2005), p. 213.

44. McCabe, *God Still Matters*, p. 35.

45. Tugwell, *Beatitudes*, pp. 94, 97.

46. Timothy Radcliffe, OP, *Why Go to Church? The Drama of the Eucharist* (Continuum, 2008), p. 18.

47. Brian Davies, OP, *Aquinas* (Continuum, 2002), p. 109.

48. Aquinas, *Summa Theologiae* (Cambridge University Press, 2006), Vol. 23, 'Virtue', edited by W.D. Hughes, q. 55.1, p. 9.

49. McCabe, *God Still Matters*, p. 29; see also p. 35.

50. Yves Congar, OP, 'Action et contemplation: D'une lettre du père Congar au père Regamey' (1959), *La vie spirituelle*, 152, 727 (1998), p. 204; quoted in Paul Murray, OP, *The New Wine of Dominican Spirituality*, p. 22.

51. McCabe, *God Still Matters*, p. 191.

52. Noffke, *Letters of Catherine of Siena*, Letter T52, to Jeronimo da Siena of the Hermits of Saint Augustine, February to April 1376, Vol. II, pp. 120–121.

53. Aquinas, *Summa Theologiae*, Vol. 24, edited by Edward D. O'Connor, CSC, q. 68.4.

54. Aquinas, *Summa Theologiae*, Vol. 36, edited by Thomas Gilby, OP, q. 52.2.

55. Congar, in Murray, *New Wine of Dominican Spirituality*, p. 23.

56. Aquinas, *Summa Theologiae*, Vol. 23, edited by W.D. Hughes, OP, q. 83.1.

57. Tugwell, *Beatitudes*, p. 96.

58. Barron, *Thomas Aquinas*, p. 154.

59. Suzanne Noffke, OP, *Prayers of Catherine of Siena* (Authors Choice, 2nd ed., 2001), Prayer 18.
60. Caryll Houselander, *The Reed of God* (Arena Lettres, 1978), p. 1.
61. Houselander, *Reed of God*, p. 1.
62. McCabe, *God Still Matters*, p. 62.
63. Radcliffe, *Why Go to Church?*, p. 16.
64. *Etty*, p. 465.
65. Radcliffe, *Why Go to Church?*, p. 6.
66. One such book is the *Three in One Bible Reference Companion* (Thomas Nelson, 1982).
67. www.vatican.va/holy_father/benedict_xvi/apost_exhortations/ documents/hf_ben-xvi_exh_20100930_verbum-domini_en.html (accessed 13 December 2010).

Bibliography

Adler, Mortimer J. *Aristotle for Everybody: Difficult Thought Made Easy*. Collier Books, 1978.

Aristotle. *Nicomachean Ethics*. Translated by Martin Ostwald. Macmillan, 1962.

Aristotle. *The Nicomachean Ethics*. Translated and Introduction by David Ross. Revised by J.L. Ackrill and J.O. Urmson. Oxford University Press, 1980.

Armstrong, A.H. *An Introduction to Ancient Philosophy*. Rowan & Allanheld, 1983.

Athanasius: The Life of Antony and the Letter to Marcellinus. Translated and Introduction by Robert C. Greg. Paulist Press, 1980.

Barron, Robert. *Thomas Aquinas: Spiritual Master*. New York: Crossroad Publishing, 1996.

Bedouelle, Guy, OP. *Saint Dominic: The Grace of the Word*. Ignatius Press, 1982.

Burton-Christie, Douglas. *The Word in the Desert: Scripture and the Quest for Holiness in Early Christian Monasticism*. Oxford University Press, 1993.

Casey, Michael. *Sacred Reading: The Ancient Art of Lectio Divina*. Liguori/Triumph, 1996.

Casey, Michael. *Toward God: The Ancient Wisdom of Western Prayer*. Liguori/Triumph, 1996.

Cassian, John. *The Conferences*. Translated and annotated by Boniface Ramsey. Paulist Press, 1997.

Catherine of Siena. *The Dialogue of St. Catherine of Siena*. Translated and Introduction by Suzanne Noffke, OP. Paulist Press, 1980.

Catherine of Siena. *The Letters of Catherine of Siena*. 2nd ed. Volume I: Letters 1–70, 2000; Volume II: Letters 71–144, 2000;

Volume III: Letters 145–230, 2007; Volume IV: Letters 231–373. Translated, Introduction and Notes by Suzanne Noffke, OP. Arizona Center for Medieval and Renaissance Studies, 2008.

Catherine of Siena. *The Prayers of Catherine of Siena.* 2nd ed. Translated and edited by Suzanne Noffke, OP. Authors Choice Press, 2001.

Cessario, Romanus, OP. *Introduction to Moral Theology.* Catholic University of America Press, 2001.

Chryssavgis, John. *In the Heart of the Desert: The Spirituality of the Desert Fathers and Mothers.* Foreword by Benedicta Ward, SLG. World Wisdom, 2003.

Davies, Brian, OP. *Aquinas.* Continuum, 2002.

Ende, Michael. *The Never-ending Story.* Dutton Children's Books, 1997.

Gascoigne, Robert, ed. *John Paul II: Legacy and Witness.* St Paul's Publications, 2007.

Harmless, William, SJ. *Desert Christians: An Introduction to the Literature of Early Monasticism.* Oxford University Press, 2004.

Hillesum, Etty. *An Interrupted Life and Letters from Westerbork.* Henry and Holt, 1996.

Hillesum, Etty. *Etty: The Letters and Diaries of Etty Hillesum 1941–1943.* Novalis, 2002.

Hopkins, Gerard Manley. *Poems and Prose.* Introduction and Notes by W.H. Gardner. Penguin Classics, 1985.

Houselander, Caryll. *The Reed of God.* Arena Lettres edition, 1978.

Journeying into God: Seven Early Monastic Lives. Translated and Introduction by Tim Vivian. Fortress Press, 1996.

Lehner, Francis C., OP, ed. *Saint Dominic: Biographical Documents.* Thomist Press, 1964.

Lives of the Desert Fathers, The. Translated by Norman Russell. Introduction by Benedicta Ward, SLG. Cistercian Publications, 1981.

Luckman, Harriet A. and Linda Kulzer, OSB, eds. *Purity of Heart in Early Ascetic and Monastic Literature: Essays in Honor of Juana Raach, OSB.* Liturgical Press, 1999.

Martin, George. *Reading Scripture as the Word of God: Practical Approaches and Attitudes*. Servant Publications, 1993.

McCabe, Herbert, OP. *God Still Matters*. Edited by Brian Davies, OP. Continuum, 2002.

Murray, Paul. *The New Wine of Dominican Spirituality: A Drink Called Happiness*. Burns & Oates, 2006.

Ponticus, Evagrius. *The Praktikos & Chapters On Prayer*. Translated, Introduction and Notes by John Eudes Bamberger, ocso. Cistercian Publications, 1981.

Radcliffe, Timothy. *Why Go to Church? The Drama of the Eucharist*. Continuum, 2008.

Raymond of Capua. *The Life of St. Catherine of Siena*. Translated by George Lamb. Tan Books, 1960.

Sherwin, Michael S., OP. *By Knowledge & By Love*. Catholic University of America Press, 2005.

Stewart, Columba, OSB. 'The Desert Fathers on Radical Self-Honesty', *Vox Benedicta* 8 no. 1 (1991):7–54.

Sayings of the Desert Fathers, The: The Alphabetical Collection, revised edn. Translated and Foreword by Benedicta Ward, SLG. Preface by Metropolitan Anthony. Cistercian Publications, 1984.

Thomas Aquinas. *Summa Theologica*. Cambridge University Press, 2006.

Tugwell, Simon, OP. *The Beatitudes: Soundings in Christian Traditions*. Templegate, 1980.

Tugwell, Simon, OP. *Ways of Imperfection: An Exploration of Christian Spirituality*. Templegate, 1985.

Tugwell, Simon, OP, ed. *The Early Dominicans: Selected Writings*. Introduction by Simon Tugwell, OP. Paulist Press, 1982.

Ward, Benedicta, SLG. *Harlots of the Desert: A Study of Repentance in Early Monastic Sources*. Cistercian Publications, 1987.